Frank Indiviglio

Newts and Salamanders

Everything about Selection, Care,
Nutrition, Diseases, Breeding, and Behavior

With 80 Photographs by Richard D. Bartlett

Illustrations by Michele Earle-Bridges

This book is dedicated to my grandfather, Frank Hill, and my uncle, Sam Apa. Through a combination of genetics, patience, and understanding, they started it all.

All inquiries should be addressed to:
Barron's Educational Series, Inc.
250 Wireless Boulevard
Hauppauge, NY 11788

International Standard Book No. 0-8120-9779-3

Library of Congress Catalog Card No. 97-1166

Library of Congress Cataloging-in-Publication Data
Indiviglio, Frank.
    Newts and salamanders: everything about selection, care, nutrition, diseases, breeding, and behavior / Frank Indiviglio ; illustrations by Michele Earle-Bridges.
        p.   cm.
    ISBN 0-8120-9779-3
    1. Newts as pets. 2. Salamanders as pets.
I. Earle-Bridges, Michele. II. Title.
SF459.N48I53   1997
639.3'785—dc21   97-1166
                                                                CIP

Printed in Hong Kong

987654321

About the Author
Frank Indiviglio is Conservation Biologist/Keeper of Reptiles and Amphibians at the Bronx Zoo/Wildlife Conservation Park. In association with the Wildlife Conservation Society, he has participated in field studies of anacondas in Venezuela, sea turtles in Costa Rica and St. Croix, and of a variety of other reptiles and amphibians throughout the hemisphere. He has written and lectured on herpetology and in con junction with Science Development, Inc. has introduced thousands of school children to a variety of fascinating animals. Mr. Indiviglio holds an M.A. in conservation biology and a J.D. from St. John's University. This is his first book for Barron's.

Acknowledgments
This book, and the experiences that gave rise to it, would not have been possible without the sacrifices an encouragement of my mother, Rita Indiviglio, and my sister, Susan Indiviglio.

I have availed myself of the expertise of the staff at the Bronx Zoo/Wildlife Conservation Park for most of my life. I am especially grateful to William Conway, General Director, James Doherty, General Curator, and John Behler, Curator of Herpetology. Bonnie Raphael, D.V.M. has been particularly generous in sharing a wealth of hard-to-find information.

I thank Lorraine Bongiorno for somehow producing a readable manuscript from reams of nightmarish hand-writing—and for maintaining a pleasant disposition throughout. I would also like to acknowledge the help of my editor Don Reis for his invaluable suggestions. Finally, special thanks are due Richard D. Bartlett, both for his thoughtful review of the manuscript and for pro-viding the brilliant photos that appear in this book.

Cover Photos
Front cover: *Pseudotriton ruber nitidus;* inside front cover: *Ambystoma maculatum;* inside back cover: *Eurycea cirrigera;* back cover: *Notophthalmus viridescens viridescens.*

Important Notes
Most, if not all salamanders produce noxious and potentially fatal skin toxins. Salamanders may also transmit harmful microorganisms to human beings. Always wash carefully after handling your speci-mens. (See page 8 for further information.) For precautions about potential electrical hazards associated with terrarium keeping, see page 50.

Contents

Top: A Japanese fire-bellied newt, Cynops pyrrhogaster; *bottom:* C. orientalis.

Preface

I was born and raised in the Bronx, New York—which may not seem the ideal place to lay the foundation for a lifelong interest in natural history. But, armed with an inquisitive mind, supported by an understanding family, and living in close proximity to both the Bronx Zoo/Wildlife Conservation Park and the American Museum of Natural History, I started early on my career path. In retrospect, the journey seems almost preordained—if somewhat convoluted at times; and I know this to have been the case for many of my colleagues, as well.

I hope that this book will contribute to your understanding of the natural history, conservation concerns, and captive husbandry of salamanders. As importantly, I hope it spurs you to further research and, perhaps, to consider a career in herpetology. Remember that most professionals started out as kids fascinated by living things; but they then went on to carry this interest a bit further than most.

Unfortunately, many herpetologists lose contact with living creatures as they rise in their profession. When such people visit at the Bronx Zoo/Wildlife Conservation Park, they observe the collections with wide-eyed wonder. Frequently, they tell me how lucky I am to spend the entire day working with live animals. Knowing this, you should attempt to share your direct observations with these "deprived" professionals. A quiet personality prevented me from doing this and hindered my entry into the field. Therefore, I urge you to attend meetings (see page 125) and speak with the people there. Lectures and articles need not be limited to topics intelligible to people with graduate degrees. Basic life histories of even the most widespread salamanders are often little known. In the text that follows, I will try to point out areas in which important contributions can be made by interested nonprofessionals.

Because most herpetologists are underfunded, many will welcome help from sincerely interested volunteers. This can lead to publications and even job opportunities. Enlist the help of local zoological parks, museums, nature centers, and libraries to find out who is working in your area. Record everything and enlist the help of children and elderly friends or relatives in studying your subjects. I have learned a great deal from the volunteers in the Bronx Zoo's Friends of Wildlife Conservation Park, most of whom had great interest and enthusiasm, but little or no formal biological training. Naturally, formal training will increase your chances of career success; but do not let the lack of it stand in the way of advancing your interest. Above all, share what you learn with others. Speaking for myself, I would be delighted to hear from you.

Frank Indiviglio
March 1997

Preliminary Considerations

Environmental Ethics

Since the late 1980s, biologists have been noting, with increasing alarm, apparent declines in a number of amphibian species worldwide. While the current research emphasis is on frogs, salamanders may be in an even worse position as they are more secretive and do not announce themselves with mating calls as do frogs.

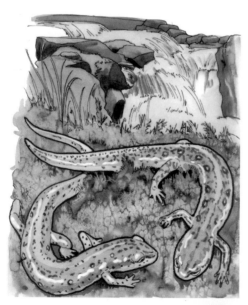

Newts and salamanders thrive in pristine environments.

Thus, we know little of the status of most salamander species. The frightening aspect of these declines is that many are unexplained by such traditional causes as overcollecting, pollution, and habitat loss. If, as some suspect, more insidious forces such as acid rain, increased exposure to ultraviolet light, or global climatic change are at work, it may already be too late for many species. With their permeable skin and dual life modes (land and water), amphibians are particularly vulnerable to change. In a sense, they serve as a "canary in the coal mine," possibly predicting a bleak future for the earth's other life forms, including ourselves.

It is therefore imperative that people keeping salamanders in captivity are certain that their specimens are captive bred. It is also vital that hobbyists study the literature in order to be able to breed those animals that they keep. Much of the necessary work can be carried out at libraries, zoos, and museums.

Given current conditions, it is a gross breach of environmental ethics for the hobbyist to collect animals in the wild. The state of the environment is such today that each animal removed from its natural habitat *does* make a difference. In addition to the outright loss of a species and the effects this has on other plants and animals, each extinction closes a door on possible cures for disease that may be locked away in the body chemistry of the extinct creature. Please read, study, visit, and support research facilities, but do *not* collect salamanders. My work at the Bronx Zoo/Wildlife Conservation Park has convinced me that serious hobbyists can make a difference by cooperating with such institutions and without disturbing natural populations. If and when collection is necessary, it should be through such institutions, and under strict government supervision.

The Law

The increased focus on disappearing amphibians and the explosion in the collection of wild animals has led to the passage of local, state, and federal laws to protect certain species. The fact that an animal is in a pet store is not an assurance that it is legal to purchase it. The prospective pet owner is responsible for researching the legality of ownership (see Useful Literature and Addresses, page 124).

Medical Research Involving Salamanders

The Mexican axolotl, *Ambystoma mexicanum*, is widely used in medical research, especially in the field of embryology.

The skin secretions of amphibians have been shown to have antimicrobial, antibiotic, and antiviral properties, and to contain chemicals with pain-killing properties. Other chemicals in amphibian skin (peptides) show promise for use in brain function and disorder research, and the mucus is being studied for use as a glue to repair damage to internal organs. The blue-spotted salamander, *Ambystoma laterale*, and other species move across snow and tolerate complete freezing of their bodies with no ill effects. The glucose and glycerol that they manufacture to prevent tissue

damage may have important applications in a variety of situations, such as organ and tissue storage.

It seems likely that the chemically active skin of salamanders will yield a variety of substances and medications that can benefit humankind. Once extinct, however, a species and its uses are forever beyond our reach.

Contributions You Can Make

As mentioned previously, cooperation with zoological parks, museums, and other institutions can provide opportunity for serious hobbyists to indulge their passion while helping preserve wild salamander populations. Such cooperation can take the form of participation in breeding programs, field studies, release programs, or surveys. Several states sponsor wildlife surveys. Some nature centers have programs to help amphibians cross roads during breeding migrations when thousands might otherwise be killed. Certain municipalities have gone as far as constructing salamander and toad tunnels to allow amphibians to pass safely under roads. And, of course, any activities that result in environmentally sound legislation will benefit a variety of creatures, including salamanders.

Turning Your Hobby into a Career

I am one of a very small number of fortunate people who is paid to do what he enjoys most—working with amphibians and reptiles. A hobby *can* become a career. In my case it took decades, sacrifice, and a good deal of help from others (to whom I remain grateful). Today, education is a necessity, overriding the importance of experience in the hiring policies of most zoological parks. Volunteering is an excellent way to add practical experience to your academic qualifications.

The fire salamander, Salamandra salamandra. *Note the pitted parotid glands.*

Warning: Skin Toxins and Disease

In the unlikely event that you wish to consume a salamander—don't!! As discussed in the section dealing with amphibian skin (see page 16), most, if not all, salamanders produce noxious and potentially fatal skin toxins. The newts of the genus *Taricha* have caused human fatalities when swallowed. The tarichotoxin that they produce, which is nearly identical to the poison of the infamous Japanese fugu fish, causes cardiac arrest. It is important that you do not handle salamanders with open cuts on your hands, lest the skin toxins enter your circulatory system. Always wash thoroughly after holding a salamander. One researcher became blind for several days when secretions from a *plethodontid* salamander entered his eye via his finger. These secretions can harm other animals as well. Even carrying cases must be rinsed, to prevent the next inhabitant from absorbing toxins left behind by a previous occupant. (I've seen frogs die after being put into a bucket that formerly held toads; the same might hold true for many salamanders.)

A variety of harmful microorganisms can be transmitted from animals to people, the most widely publicized being *salmonella.* Aquariums and utensils used in animal care should never be cleaned in sinks used for preparing human food or for washing eating utensils. Hands should be thoroughly washed, preferably with an antibacterial soap, after servicing or handling pets. One must be particularly careful with children. Make absolutely certain that they wash their hands carefully if ever they touch a specimen, and *never* allow them to put anything that may have contacted an animal into their mouths.

While the majority of salamanders cannot inflict a painful bite, the larger species should be handled with care. The amphiuma, *Amphiuma* sp., in particular can inflict a severe bite, and hungry individuals will lash out very quickly at anything in their vicinity.

Classification and Characteristics of Salamanders

Salamanders, along with frogs and caecilians, are amphibians, a class of animals that contains over 4,500 species. The exact number is open to question as new species are always being discovered and, unfortunately, are also becoming extinct as people explore and exploit their natural habitats. The nearly 400 species of salamander form the order Caudata, within the class Amphibia. The balance of the class is made up of the approximately 4,000 species of frogs (order Anura) and 163 species of caecilians (order Gymnophiona)

At first glance, the "typical" salamander superficially resembles the "typical" lizard, but a closer examination will reveal that the two animals are very dissimilar. The specifics of the differences should become clear as you read on. Salamanders themselves exhibit a surprising array of physical forms and lifestyles, and range in size from the diminutive Mexican lungless salamander, *Thorius pennatulas*, which is full grown at 1.5 inches (3.8 cm) long, to the Japanese and Chinese giant salamanders, *Andrias japonicus* and *A. davidianus*, which measure in excess of 5 feet (1.5 m). There are colorless, eyeless cave salamanders, arboreal species, eel-like animals with only two legs, as well as species that never undergo metamorphosis and breed in the larval form. Among these animals one can find species that guard their eggs, others that give birth to fully developed miniatures of themselves, and some that walk across the snow to lay their eggs in frigid ponds. All of these variations in lifestyle and form will be discussed in greater detail later in the book.

The Various Families of Salamanders

All salamanders belong to the order Caudata, which is divided into nine families containing 62 genera. The order is sometimes split into three suborders: the Cryptobranchoidea, containing the more primitive giant salamanders or Cryptobranchidae and the stream-dwelling Asiatic Hynobiidae; the Salamandroidae, comprised of seven families of what the reader may consider "typical" salamanders (although many are actually quite strange in appearance and habits); and the Sirenoidea, whose sole members are the aquatic, two-legged sirens. So unique are the sirens that some authors have proposed placing them in a separate order, the Meantes.

Family Cryptobranchidae— the Giant Salamanders

This family contains the largest of all salamanders, the Chinese giant salamander, *Andrias davidianus*, which grows to lengths in excess of 5 feet

(1.5 m). The Japanese giant salamander, *A. japonicus*, grows nearly as large. The only other species in the family, the hellbender, belongs to a separate genus, *Cryptobranchus*, and is native to the northeastern and central United States. Although dwarfed by its Asian relatives, the stockily built hellbender reaches the impressive length of 28 inches (71.1 cm), and is the heaviest and among the longest of the North American salamanders. All three species inhabit clear, cool streams, usually with moving water, and are totally aquatic. Evolution in pristine environments has most likely predisposed these animals to problems when those environments are altered, and indeed all are in some degree of trouble in the wild. These animals undergo a form of incomplete metamorphosis in which lungs develop but gill slits are retained, and eyelids do not form. They have loose folds of "extra" skin to provide as large a surface as possible for oxygen absorption, but can also rise to the surface and breathe via the lungs. The giant salamanders remain under rocks or other cover by day, and feed on aquatic creatures such as fish, snails, crayfish, worms, and other salamanders. There is circumstantial evidence that the Chinese giant salamander may even take prey as large as ducks. Smell and possibly the sense of touch are probably more important than eyesight in locating prey and mates.

The giant salamanders and the hynobiids are the only species known to utilize external fertilization. Males of all three species hollow out a space beneath a rock and allow several gravid females to lay eggs there. Other males are chased from the area. The resident male releases sperm over the eggs after they have been laid, and guards them until they hatch in two and one-half to three months. Larvae disperse upon hatching and are able to fend for themselves.

Family Hynobiidae—the Asiatic Salamanders

The nine genera of hynobiids contain approximately 35 species. The range of the Siberian salamander, *Salamandrella keyserlingi*, extends into eastern Europe; all of the other species are confined to Asia, and are found as far east as Japan and Taiwan. The hynobiids are average-sized salamanders, the largest reaching 10 inches (25.4 cm) in length. The lungs are very small or absent, which seems to restrict them to living in or near cool streams, where oxygen levels are usually high. They tend to be terrestrial, but the eggs are laid in water. As with the Cryptobranchidae, and in contrast to all other families, fertilization of the eggs is external. The female lays two gelatinous packets, each of which contains up to 70 eggs. The male presses these egg capsules to his cloaca and releases sperm on them. The males of several species have been observed to guard the eggs throughout incubation. Unique among the salamanders are those *Hynobius* that have claws, the function of which is as yet unknown. The genera in the family Hynobiidae are *Onychodactylus*, *Pachypalaminus*, *Salamandrella*, *Hynobius*, *Ranodon*, *Liuia*, *Batrachuperus*, and *Pachyhynobius*.

Family Salamandridae—the Brook Salamanders, Fire Salamanders, and Newts

The approximately 55 species (14 genera) of salamandrids contain animals that come to mind when most people hear the words "salamander" and "newt." Members of this family can be found in the western and eastern United States, Europe, Asia, and even the northern parts of Africa—a continent largely devoid of salamanders. The salamandridae are the only members of the suborder *Salamandroidea* that lack rib grooves along the sides of the body. Those animals in this group that are termed "newts" generally spend about half of the year in water, while some have a distinct larval aquatic stage, land stage (during which they are termed "efts") and finally a fully aquatic adult phase. Upon their return to water, several radical physical changes occur. The skin becomes thinner and smoother to facilitate oxygen transfer, and the tail and eyes change shape to aid swimming and allow for underwater vision. Lateral line organs, important for orientation and prey location, also develop, and the rear feet of some species become webbed. The alpine salamander, *Salamandra atra*, gives birth to completely metamorphosed young. Some populations of the fire salamander, *Salamandra salamandra*, also utilize this method of reproduction, while others give birth to larvae.

Among this family there are several species that demonstrate an incredibly accurate ability to return to home ranges or breeding ponds, perhaps using polarized light that strikes the pineal body, sensing of the earth's magnetic fields, or some as yet unknown mechanism. The red-bellied newt, *Taricha rivularis*, in particular, seems to possess extraordinary abilities in this regard. This resident of western North America has been observed to return to its breeding pond after being transported nine miles away. What makes this fact all the more extraordinary is that the small animals had to cross high mountains and streams, some of which were the breeding habitat of other newts of the same species. Representative genera include *Taricha*, *Triturus*, *Euproctus*, *Chioglossa*, *Pleurodeles* and *Salamandra*.

The crested newt, Triturus cristatus. *This member of the family Salamandridae is found in central and eastern Europe. The male (top) develops a dorsal crest during the breeding season.*

Family Amphiumidae— the Amphiumas or "Congo Eels"

This family contains three species of salamander in one genus, all of which live in the southeastern United States. The two-toed amphiuma, *Amphiuma means*, reaches a length of 46 inches (117 cm), and is thus the longest salamander in the Western Hemisphere. The amphiumas have four tiny legs that are apparently useless for locomotion. The number of toes on the feet varies, and gives the three species their common names: the one-toed amphiuma, *Amphiuma pholeter*, the two-toed amphiuma, *Amphiuma means,* and the three-toed amphiuma, *A. tridactylum*. They are almost completely aquatic, and retain certain larval characteristics, such as gill slits and the absence of eyelids.

The giant salamanders, family Cryptobranchidae, include only two genera and three species. This juvenile hellbender, Cryptobranchus alleganiensis, *is native to the northeastern and central United States.*

Amphiumas have been seen to leave the water on wet, rainy nights and gravid females seek shelter on damp land near water. The female coils

The brook salamanders, fire salamanders, and newts, family Salamandridae, include 14 genera and approximately 55 species. An Alpine newt, Triturus alpestrus, *is shown in a beautifully arranged aquarium.*

around her eggs (which may number nearly 200) for the entire incubation period of five months. The male transfers sperm directly into the female's cloaca. The larvae develop functional legs, but adults move by eellike undulations of the body.

Family Proteidae—Mudpuppies and the Olm

The two genera in this family contain six species. Five are mudpuppies, genus *Necturus*, and the other genus is comprised of one species, the olm, *Proteus anguinus*. The olm is a truly unusual creature, being found only in subterranean pools and streams in the western Balkan Peninsula and northern Italy. Its skin lacks pigment and it is totally blind, the tiny eyes being buried below the skin. Gills are external and lungs are present in adults. Olms appear to utilize two breeding strategies, sometimes eggs (15 to 65) are laid beneath a stone and guarded by both parents, while on other occasions the female gives birth to one or two well-developed larvae. The developing larvae are nourished by eggs that break down within the female's body.

The mudpuppies, or waterdogs, have external gills and lungs, and are found in eastern and central North America. The size of the gills is influenced by the oxygen content of the water in which they live. Animals from cool, well-oxygenated waters have smaller gills than those from still, southern swamps. Mudpuppies are aquatic, feeding on nearly any small animal they can catch. Males guard eggs for the incubation period, which may be up to two months in the northern portion of their range.

Family Ambystomatidae— the Mole Salamanders

The 35 species (four genera) of salamanders in this family are generally stoutly built, burrowing creatures. Most have a dark brown or black background color, and are boldly patterned in contrasting stripes, spots, or blotches. The family is restricted to North America. The common name, mole salamander, arises from the burrowing lifestyle of these animals. As adults, they lead a subterranean existence, emerging from their underground retreats only to breed or perhaps, for short feeding forays. Many species of mole salamander breed in late winter or early spring. The spotted salamander, *Ambystoma maculatum*, has been observed crawling across snow to reach its breeding pond. The marbled salamander, *Ambystoma opacum*, lays eggs in dried pond beds in the fall. The female remains coiled around the eggs until rising water levels stimulate hatching. Ambystomids always begin life as aquatic larvae and usually transform into terrestrial adults. Some populations of tiger salamanders, *Ambystoma tigrinum*, however, exhibit paedomorphism and reproduce without transforming into adult form. The Mexican axolotl, *Ambystoma mexicanum*, on the other hand, never transforms into a terrestrial adult, and breathes using both gills and lungs. Some subspecies of the tiger salamander, *Ambystoma tigrinum*, can reach lengths in excess of 1 foot (30 cm), making them the largest of the North American terrestrial salamanders.

The "Congo eels" are members of the family Amphiumidae, which consists of one genus with three species—each distinguished by the number of its toes. The one-toed amphiuma, Amphiuma pholeter, *is shown here.*

never transforms into a terrestrial adult. In contrast to most other salamanders, the Pacific giant salamander will emit noises when disturbed.

Family Dicamptodontidae— the Pacific Mole Salamanders

The three species (two genera) were formerly classified as family Ambystomatidae. The Pacific giant salamander, *Dicamptodon ensatus*, rivals the tiger salamander, *Ambystoma tigrinum*, in size, and resembles it in body form. These animals are found only in or near cool mountain streams along the northwest coast of the United States. One, Cope's giant salamander, *Diacamptodon copei*, is neotenic, and

The family Proteidae consists of two genera that contain a total of six species—five of which are mudpuppies. This one, Necturus maculosus, *is found in the eastern parts of Canada and the United States.*

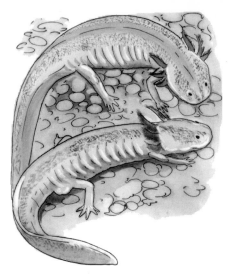

Mexican axolotls, Ambystoma mexicanum, *are nearly extinct in the wild. The female (top) and male (bottom) are shown.*

Family Plethodontidae— the Lungless Salamanders

This largest salamander family (about 245 species in 30 genera) is also considered to be the most evolutionarily advanced. Among these animals we find many unique adaptations and lifestyles. They alone possess the nasolabial groove, a structure that, by a type of capillary action, carries odors from the damp earth to the nose. All members of this family lack lungs and most are without gills. They breathe through the skin and lining of the mouth. As the skin must be moist for respiration to occur, lungless salamanders must live in damp places, and can emerge only on cool, wet nights. They are also fairly small in size. The largest reaches about 8 inches (20 cm) and most are considerably smaller. The small size allows for a greater surface area in proportion to volume, and thus increases respira-

tory efficiency. Their lifestyles are a study in diversity. Many lungless salamanders hatch from terrestrial eggs as mini-adults, while others are pale, gilled creatures with vestigial eyes that never leave the underground streams in which they are born. The grotto salamander, *Typhlotriton spelaeus,* begins life as a typical larvae but migrates into subterranean cave pools upon metamorphosis. There it loses its gills and skin pigment and the eyes become covered with skin. The skin secretions of several lungless salamanders are quite sticky, and may function to gum up the jaws of snakes or other predators. Many terrestrial forms appear to be territorial, marking and defending a specific home range. The extremely porous skins of the Plethodontids predispose them to severe problems when pollutants are introduced into their habitats. Many species are becoming increasingly uncommon, but may still appear in the pet trade due to local availability. This is currently the case for the two-lined salamander, *Eurycea bislineata,* and the long-tailed salamander, *Eurycea longicauda.* Because they are fairly delicate animals, neither should be kept until one has worked with other small but more common species, such as the red-backed salamander, *Plethodon cinereus,* or the dusky salamander, *Desmognathus fuscus.* Representative genera include *Eurycea, Batrachoseps, Desmognathus,* and *Plethodon.*

Family Sirenidae—the Sirens

As stated earlier, the sirens are so unique among the salamanders that some taxonomists have suggested creating a separate order for them. Sirens inhabit slow-moving bodies of water in the eastern and central United States and in northeastern Mexico. They are completely aquatic, have lungs and external gills, and lack rear legs. The front legs are tiny and located far up the body, near the gills. The body is long and eellike. Eyelids are lacking. The greater siren, *Siren lacertina*, reaches a length of 37 inches (94 cm), and is thus one of the longest of the salamanders. The dwarf siren, *Pseudobranchus striatus*, is barely 10 inches (25 cm) long. A puzzling aspect of siren biology is their mode of egg fertilization, which is as yet unknown. The male lacks the normal glands that make spermatophores, and the females are without spermatophore storage receptacles, so it is assumed that fertilization is external; however, the eggs are laid singly or in small clumps. (If external fertilization is practiced, the male would have to accompany the female while laying and individually fertilize each egg, a heretofore undescribed reproduction strategy.) Also unusual is the ability of some species to undergo aestivation when their watery habitat dries out. The thick mucus covering on the skin hardens and forms a type of cocoon around the animal, with an opening at the mouth. Sirens can wait out droughts of several months duration in this state.

Characteristics of Salamanders

Sight

The importance of sight varies among the salamanders. Some, such as the lungless salamanders (family Plethodontidae) have binocular vision (unique among amphibians), while others function quite well without any eyes at all (the olm, *Proteus anguinus*). As with many other animals, the pupil contracts and dilates according to prevailing light levels. In contrast to other animals, the eyes are focused by moving the lens rather than by changing its shape. Some species can distinguish eight different colors, and acuity is such that many can see their prey in near-total darkness. (The American toad, *Bufo americanus*, will recognize and avoid bees and bee mimics after being stung; color may be its recognition cue. I am unaware of experiments demonstrating such an ability in salamanders, although the ability may exist.) With the exception of permanently aquatic species, all salamanders have movable eyelids.

Hearing

Although they lack eardrums, salamanders have a complex inner ear system. It would therefore seem to follow that the ability to hear is important to them, but, unfortunately, little work has been done in this area. The available research seems to indicate that salamanders hear low frequency sounds, and that the inner ear is sensitive to ground-borne vibrations as well.

The lateral line: As an alternative way of "hearing," highly aquatic salamanders have a lateral line system by which they monitor water movement and detect predators and prey. The lateral line is a series of pitlike depressions containing hair cells or mechanoreceptive neuromasts, and is located along the head and sides of the animal. The lateral line system may also contain ampullary organs—electroreceptors that help the salamander orient itself, find prey, and escape predators.

Sense of Smell

Salamanders sense chemical aspects of their environment through two systems: the olfactory system (similar to the sense of smell in other animals), and the vomeronasal system. The olfactory system assists in many activities: species and individual recognition, courtship, recognition of home territory, and, for some species, feeding. The vomeronasal sense is used to sample chemical cues from substances in the mouth. Lungless salamanders have a second way of using this sense. Small canals in each side of the snout

The mole salamanders, family Ambystom-atidae, consist of 35 species in four genera. A female marbled salamander, Ambystoma opacum *is seen guarding her nest.*

(nasolabial grooves) draw fluids across the vomeronasal organ (Jacobson's organ). In this way, female red-backed salamanders, *Plethodon cinereus*, test

The lungless salamanders, family Plethodontidae, include about 245 species in 30 genera. Plethodon jordani *numbers several subspecies, some of which have red cheeks or red legs, while others are quite nondescript.*

the feces of males to determine the quality of their diet and presumably, their fitness as mates.

The Skin

Salamander skin is supplied with a variety of granular, or poison, glands, whose secretions are distasteful to predators and that are potentially fatal if swallowed (see warning on page 8). A California newt, *Taricha torosa*, under my care lived for 12 years in an aquarium with an American eel, *Anguilla anguilla*. The eel would consume everything that entered its domain (including the hand that fed it, if allowed!), yet ignored the newt (and an African clawed frog, *Xenopus laevis*) completely. Perhaps it had taken a sample bite or perhaps a chemical cue warned it to avoid the toxic creature. In any event, the eel's strategy worked, for it enjoyed a variety of other meals for 17 years. Eastern newts of the genus *Notophthalmus* have the poison in smaller quantities.

Other skin glands release mucus to prevent dessication, aid in respiration, and repel harmful microorganisms. Males of some species have glands that, during the breeding season, release pheromones that attract females.

Shedding: As with all amphibians, salamanders periodically shed their skin. The old skin splits around the mouth and is peeled back toward the tail. In most cases the salamander eats the old skin, obtaining some nourishment in the process.

The skin's function in the respiratory process will be discussed in the next section.

Respiration

Salamanders have evolved a wide array of breathing strategies, far more than any other group of creatures. Depending upon the species, respiration is accomplished through the skin, gills, lungs, membranes of the mouth and throat, or a combination thereof. Those that breathe with lungs or throat membranes use throat pulsations (buccopharyngeal movements) to force air or water over or into these structures. The lungless salamanders (Plethodontidae) breathe entirely through their skin (cutaneous respiration), and even those with gills and/or lungs use this method to some degree. Some aquatic species such as the hellbender, *Cryptobranchus alleganiensis*, have wrinkled skin folds that they move about to increase their effective respiratory surface.

Reproduction

Salamanders use an incredible array of mating strategies; I will attempt here only a brief overview. Greater detail will be given under the various species accounts (beginning on page 171) and in the section concerning natural history (beginning on page 19).

Breeding is seasonal in most temperate species, and is initiated by rainfall, an increase in day length or temperature, or a combination of these factors. Tropical species may breed throughout the year. Fertilization is, with few exceptions, internal. The male deposits a sperm packet (spermatophore), which the female takes into her cloaca. The male may guide her to the spermatophore using an embrace (amplexus) or a form of controlled walking until she is directly over the sperm packet. The salamanders that utilize external fertilization (Hynobiidae, Cryptobranchidae) do so in water, with the male releasing sperm directly onto the eggs. Males may attract females by releasing pheromones or, in some cases by elaborate displays. Males of some newts (genus *Triturus*) develop enlarged dorsal fins to facilitate such displays. Eggs may be deposited and abandoned (in water), guarded in water, or guarded on land.

The sirens, family Sirenidae, are completely aquatic. The lesser siren, Siren intermedia, *ranges throughout the southern and central United States.*

Larvae hatching from aquatic eggs typically have external gills and, for a time, balancers, which are thin structures that prop the animal up from the mud at the pond's bottom, presumably to keep the gills clean. They are carnivorous, and, in contrast to tadpoles,

An adult hellbender, Cryptobranchus alleganiensis, *eating its recently shed skin.*

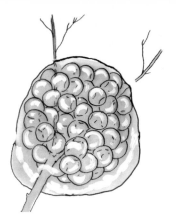

The eggs of the spotted salamander, Ambystoma maculatum, *are laid very early in the spring.*

A marbled salamander, Ambystoma opacum, *guarding her eggs.*

the front limbs appear first. Gills are typically resorbed upon metamorphosis and tail fins are lost.

Neoteny: Certain species exhibit neoteny, a process wherein metamorphosis is not attained. Such animals, in effect, become sexually mature and breed while still larvae. Neoteny or paedomorphosis is usually associated with cold waters and may occur occasionally or always, depending on the species and the population.

Terrestrial eggs give rise to fully formed larvae. The fire salamander, *Salamandra salamandra*, gives birth to a larvae with four legs and gills, and some populations are born fully formed (miniature adults).

The larvae of the marbled salamander, *Ambystoma opacum*, and the tiger salamander, *A. Tigrinum*, have been shown to select nonrelated larvae as prey, and thus exhibit kin recognition.

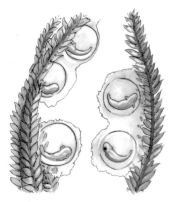

The Mexican axolotl, Ambystoma mexicanum, *will attach her eggs to water plants or any other substrate within the tank.*

Larvae of the tiger salamander, Ambystoma tigrinum. *The newly hatched larvae feed ravenously and mature quickly. The full-grown specimen (bottom) is almost ready to leave the pond.*

Understanding Newts and Salamanders

General Activity

The following sections should be considered against the backdrop of each particular species' entire life cycle; viewing an activity pattern in isolation will leave us with a distorted view of the animals' needs in captivity.

Salamanders usually utilize quite different habitats at various life stages and times of the year. The marbled salamander, *Ambystoma opacum*, for example, uses different habitats as aquatic larvae and a terrestrial adult; however, "terrestrial" is too general a term to describe the needs of this animal. In the warmer months, adults are mainly below ground, feeding and varying the depth and location of burrowing with temperature and moisture levels. In the fall, gravid females journey to a dried pond basin. There the eggs are laid and guarded until rising water levels (in late winter) stimulate hatching. The females probably do not feed during this time; they leave this area for other terrestrial haunts after the eggs hatch. Larvae also vary their aquatic habitat depending on food availability, temperature, light levels, and a host of other factors (chemical makeup of the water, competition, etc.), of which we know little. The skilled (and lucky) keeper can often modify and manipulate the animals' needs so that they are met in artificial (and usually smaller) surroundings, but the overall scheme of the salamanders' natural history must be adhered to. The "nuts and bolts" of such modifications and manipulations will take up most of the rest of this book.

Feeding Behavior

Salamanders are carnivorous. Some plant and fungal material has been found in the stomachs of several species, but it is probable that this was taken incidentally, while feeding on living prey. While sight seems to be the most important feeding cue, especially among terrestrial species, I have observed the tiger salamander, *Ambystoma tigrinum*, consuming non-moving insect prey. A wide variety of species that feed in water will take

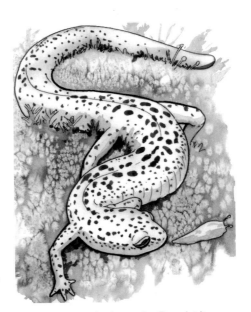

The Northern red salamander, Pseudotriton ruber ruber, *is found in the open only on cool, wet nights.*

Hellbenders thrive in unpolluted rivers and streams in the eastern third of the United States.

food such as bits of meat and fish flakes and pellets. This food is taken rapidly and with little or no preconditioning, so I imagine that such species may rely on scent when hunting in their natural habitats as well. Cave-dwelling species, some of which are blind, also appear to rely heavily on scent in locating prey.

Lateral line: Water movements detected by the lateral line (see Hearing, page 15) are relied upon by aquatic species. I have observed African clawed frogs, *Xenopus laevis* (an aquatic frog with a lateral line system), responding to a pen tapping on aquarium glass even when black paper hid the pen's movement from the frog's vision. Water-borne vibrations are the most likely stimulus, and may also be sensed by salamanders possessing lateral line sensory pits. Electroreceptors (ampullary organs) are also present in the lateral lines of some salamanders but their function is not completely understood at this time.

Diet variation: Salamanders vary their diet seasonally and, in accor-

dance with activity levels, nutritional needs and a host of less understood factors. Many have been shown to selectively choose prey of a certain size or type at various times of the year. In captivity, I have not noticed salamanders lose interest in a specific food item that is offered exclusively over a long period of time (as has been shown to be the case for chameleons). Nutritional considerations for captive salamanders at the various life cycle stages are discussed in the chapter on Nutrition (page 51).

Teeth: Most salamanders have replaceable, loosely bound teeth in both jaws and, depending on the species, in the roof of the mouth. The teeth hold rather than chew the prey, although a crushing function also appears evident, especially in large species consuming sizable prey items. Some species can shoot the tongue out to capture small prey a considerable distance away (nearly half the snout-vent length). Other species appear to grab the prey with their jaws only, but close examination will reveal that the sticky, mucus-coated tongue is also playing a role in the capture.

Eyes: Terrestrial salamanders retract their eyes into the sockets when swallowing, a behavior thought by some to assist in pushing the food down the throat.

Territoriality and Home Range Orientation

Terrestrial salamanders, as far as is known, generally keep to a home range in which most of their needs can be fulfilled. This area can range in size from a 3 or 4 to over 100 square feet (30 sq. m), depending upon the species. The home range, once established, is generally left only for breeding migrations or out of necessity (competition, lack of food, weather patterns). This area may be vigorously defended by posturing or actual ttack, and may be marked by glandular secretions and feces.

Salamanders that undertake breeding migrations can orient back to some ranges several hundred yards away, and experimentally displaced newts (genus *Taricha*) have returned to their territories when moved several miles. All amphibians studied thus far have a pineal body that contains photoreceptors. Light polarization and perhaps celestial cues are sensed by this organ. The actual area of reception is a patch of translucent skin, generally located between the eyes. This "third eye" probably assists the animal in its daily and seasonal movements. The sense of smell appears also to be involved in movement orientation in some species, although direct evidence is not yet available.

Recreating Nature in the Terrarium

Having looked briefly at some aspects of natural history, it seems appropriate that we discuss the role of such considerations in captive management. It is common practice to attempt to replicate an animal's natural habitat in captivity but such an undertaking is not possible. Factors touched on in the previous section, and countless others, render it impossible to create, even in a huge enclosure, something similar to a "mini swamp or pond." This is not to say that we cannot create realistic, aesthetically pleasing terrariums that allow the inhabitants to exhibit a wide range of natural behaviors and to reproduce. We can, but indulging the fantasy that we have a functioning ecosystem in a glass container will color our observations and hinder the learning process.

The specifics of what can be accomplished will be explained under the species' accounts (beginning on page 71). Here, it is sufficient to realize that the various factors that affect salamanders can be scaled down and manipulated so that, in some cases, many of the animals' natural activities can be observed. For certain types, the exact seasonal lengths and changes may be necessary for successful reproduction, and such species may not breed under captive conditions unless they are confined outdoors in their native habitats. For others, a very short, reasonable facsimile of normal seasonal changes may be enough. I'm reminded here of an amusing tale about a group of large South American river turtles (*Podocnemis* sp.) that were kept in a zoo for 30 years, healthy but not reproductively active. One day someone completely emptied their large pond (not normal practice) and refilled it. All of the turtles copulated, apparently stimulated by the dry/wet season cycle of one day! Humidity, light cycles, and food availability and type are other factors that we can manipulate in captivity.

It would seem that the closest we can come to imitating nature is to house small species in large outdoor enclosures within their natural range; for others, we must study and experiment.

A hellbender, Cryptobranchus alleganiensis, *in its native habitat in North Carolina.*

HOW-TO:
Interpreting the Behavior of Captive Salamanders

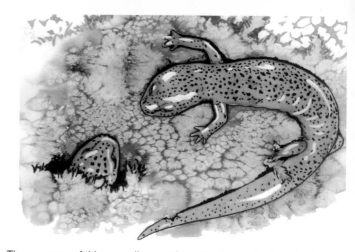

Signs of Illness

A universal difficulty faced by zookeepers is detecting sickness or injury in captive animals early enough so that medical intervention is likely to succeed. It is usually in a sick animal's best interests to appear healthy and alert, so as to not draw the attention of predators that tend to single out partially disabled prey. My experience with captive animals ranging from ants to elephants has taught me that amphibians, and in particular the more secretive salamanders, present challenging difficulties in that regard. Salamanders are generally inactive, with hours spent in one position, often hidden, and their food intake is fairly small as compared to other creatures. Therefore, clues of illness, indicated in other animals by activity levels, posture, and appetite

The presence of this normally secretive red salamander, Pseudotriton ruber, *in an unsheltered area may indicate that it has been evicted from its burrow by a more aggressive tankmate.*

are minimal. Nevertheless, though less in evidence, they can be detected.

Posture: With experience, one can often tell an ailing salamander by how it arranges itself while at rest. Subtle differences in limb and head position and alertness are detectable once you know what to look for but the changes are minute and virtually invisible to the untrained eye.

Location of the animal is important as many species are quite regular in their choice of shelters, feeding areas, etc. If a salamander relinquishes its preferred location, competition from cagemates is one possible reason. A terrestrial animal that spends most of the time in its water dish is probably telling you that the terrarium is too dry.

The splayed-out posture of this tiger salamander, Ambystoma tigrinum, *may indicate a health or an environmental problem.*

Terrestrial species, like this red salamander, may seek out a bowl of water if the conditions in the terrarium become too dry.

22

Rapid throat pulsations may indicate that a salamander is experiencing heat stress.

chemical imbalances may cause agitated movements, especially in aquatic species. This may be accompanied by rubbing movements of the feet along the body. Low oxygen levels will result in rapid waving of the external gills. (The behavioral symptoms of specific diseases will be covered under the section dealing with health beginning on page 60). Often, behaviors such as those just mentioned are most useful as warnings that a closer look at the animals and their enclosure is required.

Signs of Breeding Readiness

Restless animals may indicate the onset of breeding condition, or that a female is gravid. This may be accompanied by a loss of appetite. There are sometimes physical changes in the salamander's appearance that also signal readiness to breed. These will be explained in detail when breeding methods are discussed in the species accounts section beginning on page 71.

Movement: The salamanders' movements are also of diagnostic value; for example, most burrowing, nocturnal species will come out in the day and move about on the surface when heat stressed. Overheating might also be signaled by an increase in the movements of the throat due to a faster breathing rate. Movement at odd times may also indicate that an individual is being harassed by a tankmate, or is not getting enough food. Inappropriate pH levels or other

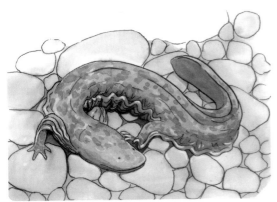

The scratching movements of this hellbender, Cryptobranchus alleganiesis, *may indicate a problem with water quality.*

Rapid gill movements, here displayed by a Mexican axolotl, may indicate a low oxygen level.

Habitats for Captive Salamanders

Woodland Terrariums

A wide variety of land-dwelling species can be housed in a woodland terrarium. Slight modification can allow for accommodation of those animals requiring a wetter habitat than that typically needed by the more completely terrestrial forms. Strictly speaking, a woodland terrarium is set up to resemble conditions in a temperate forest: moderate temperatures, areas of light and dark, damp soil covered by dead leaves and moss, and a variety of shelters in the form of rocks and logs. Most terrestrial salamanders that dwell in this environment can be maintained without standing water (except during the breeding season) if humidity is kept high and damp retreats are provided. Standing water may be provided as a safety measure, in case the terrarium should inadvertently dry out. This is best accomplished by using a water bowl. Be sure that the terrarium's inhabitants can easily exit the bowl; most are not good swimmers. Some rocks or sticks should also be placed in the bowl to prevent crickets and other food insects from drowning.

Substrate

The substrate used will vary, depending upon your approach to cleaning and the size of the enclosure. For a large, well-planted terrarium with few inhabitants, a semipermanent setup may be created using soil and moss as a substrate. Be aware, however, that the soil must be changed from time to time, and the more complex the terrarium, the harder this is to accomplish. If the tank is not crowded, it is possible to remove and replace the top layers of earth without disturbing the overall setup. Where greater numbers of animals are kept, or in smaller enclosures, complete substrate changes must be made. In such situations, it is best to use sphagnum or peat moss as the main substrate, which can be easily taken out and replaced. If the moss is arranged between rocks and wood and covered with some dead leaves, an aesthetically pleasing and easily cleaned terrarium can be created without soil. In more elaborate, permanent setups, a layer of gravel and charcoal should

A woodland terrarium. The enlargement shows that layers of moss, soil, charcoal, and gravel have been used to form the substrate.

ine the bottom of the tank. If soil is used, a little experimentation will help determine the proper consistency for burrowing animals. Many species will establish permanent retreats if the soil allows. This aids in checking on animals and provides opportunities for interesting behavioral observations. Some sphagnum moss mixed into the soil will improve moisture retention, and help prevent the soil from becoming packed. If you collect your own soil, it would be wise to test the pH as acid rain is lowering the pH of many soils to a point where salamanders may become ill or die if confined on them.

Humidity can be controlled by the type of substrate (sphagnum moss will hold a great deal of water) and by providing shelters that retain dampness. A glass cover over the screen cover is rarely necessary and the resulting stagnant air has been implicated in health problems.

Shelter

Many salamanders can be habituated to using a shelter that is alongside the glass, to allow for easier viewing. This is particularly effective if the glass-sided shelter is the only or most desirable area in which to hide. For particularly shy animals, black paper can be taped to the glass and removed when viewing is desired, or it can be removed for gradually increasing times each day until the salamander remains in the shelter without it.

Lighting

Lighting will generally be subdued, so live plants must be chosen accordingly. The subjects of lighting, temperature, and plants will be discussed under separate headings.

Water Areas

For those species naturally occurring in swamp or bog environments, or

The marbled salamander, Ambystoma opacum, *will thrive in a properly managed woodland terrarium.*

in the wet areas along streams, wet sphagnum moss or carpet moss is an ideal substrate. Many of these animals (see species accounts) will be quite at home in this medium, with a bit of a water reserve at the tank's bottom. In this situation, a separate water area or pool will not be necessary. If it is necessary or desirable, the moss can be piled up to form a "land" area without using rocks or soil. The only drawback is that moss will often impart a brownish color to the water. This can be avoided by creating a separate land area using silicone to attach a piece of plastic across one portion of the tank, or by using a plastic container, set within the aquarium, to contain the moss and keep it from contact with the water. Again, be certain that the salamanders can easily exit the water areas. If they are unable to, many will exhaust themselves trying and eventually drown. You can be certain that this will happen at a time when you are not nearby to rescue the unfortunate creature. Moss in contact with water may also clog or shut down any mechanical filtering system you may use. The previously described methods, or installing an undergravel filter (see page 39), will eliminate this as a consideration.

Shoreline Terrariums

In the shoreline terrarium we will concentrate mainly on animals such as newts, which spend a good deal of time in the water but need a terrestrial resting and hiding place. These animals are mainly classified in the family *Salamandridae*. Many attractive and interesting members of this family can be bred in captivity in a shoreline terrarium, including the Pacific newts of the genus *Taricha*, the alpine newt, *Triturus alpestis*, the red-spotted newt, *Notopthalmus viridescens*, and the sharp-ribbed newt, *Pleurodeles waltl* (see individual species accounts for specifics).

Since newts are generally well adapted to an aquatic existence, water can be quite deep for some species, provided, again, that egress is uncomplicated. Many can even be housed in a fairly deep aquarium with a floating

A shoreline terrarium. Fairly deep water with easy access to a dry surface is essential for newts that require both aquatic and a terrestrial environments.

piece of cork bark as the only land area. Floating plastic or live plants can also be used. In fairly aquatic situations, it is important to be sure that the outflow from your filtration is not too strong. Most newts are not strong swimmers, and the constant stress of battling a current to reach the surface will quickly weaken and kill them. Too rapid a water flow will also interfere with proper feeding. Most species are fairly slow and deliberate feeders, often taking time to smell the prey before consuming it. Using an undergravel filter is probably the safest and most effective approach to take in this situation. The outflow can be directed upwards so as not to create dangerous currents while still allowing for highly effective biological filtration. The gravel used should be too large to be swallowed. Certain aquatic creatures can pass small stones while others cannot, so it is best to err on the side of caution. Blackworms introduced into the aquarium will burrow into the gravel and keep the salamanders occupied with hunting. Just be sure the salamanders are getting enough to eat if blackworms are a main component of their diet. Blackworms will thrive at the cool temperatures required to keep most newts healthy.

Wood

Ironwood, coralwood, monkeywood, or other types of dense, sinking woods make excellent land areas. In a deep-water tank, they are especially useful in that newts can climb up the branching support areas on their way to the surface of the water. Their twisted, gnarled structure is aesthetically pleasing and also increases surface area in the aquarium. The smooth wood is an ideal substrate on which the animals can rest.

Gravel

The delicate skin of these amphibious creatures dictates that we avoid sharp or rough stone in their aquariums. Smooth, rounded gravel or pebbles are acceptable, as long as they cannot be swallowed by the aquariums inhabitants. For those animals that require a great deal of water but also use land for shelter, as opposed to just resting (for example, the sharp-ribbed newt, *Pleurodeles waltl*; see individual species accounts for others), a land area can be fashioned from mounds of gravel. Several mounds of different heights can add interest to the setup. Plants such as pothos and devil's ivy, which will thrive in wet gravel, can be used to provide hiding places and also serve well as aquatic "ladders," enabling the newts to reach the surface of the water easily.

Gravel cleaning: Even with effective filtration, gravel cleaning is a necessity (see Filtration, page 39) for more details. Siphon tubes with one end wider than the other, sold as "gravel washers," serve quite well in elaborate aquariums that cannot be easily broken down and rinsed. Gravel is sucked partway up the tube but remains in the aquarium, while debris is flushed out. There are even battery-operated models available, but the manual ones work quite well.

Covers

Although quite definitely aquatic creatures, newts (and other salamanders) exhibit a remarkable ability to crawl up glass. For this reason, a secure cover is a must. Most cannot survive long on the floor, and usually desiccate before one can recover them.

Aquariums (Aquatic Terrariums)

Wholly aquatic species require that modification be made to the basics of amphibian keeping. Land-dwelling animals can, if the enclosure is large enough, move away from areas that are soiled with waste products; however, once aquarium water is fouled, the ani-mal has no way to move to a more suitable area. Animals such as the *Amphiuma* sps. the *Siren* sps., the mudpuppy, *Necturus maculosus*, and of course the various giant salamanders, the hellbender, *Cryptobranchus alleganiensis*, and the Japanese and Chinese giant salamanders, *Andrias japonicas* and *A. davidiensis*, are a challenge because of their size and the volume of waste products they produce.

Waste Products

Water quality is a paramount issue for all aquarium species, as they are confined to the same water into which they excrete their waste products. The skin is generally extremely porous, and allows for easy transport of not only oxygen but harmful pollutants as well. Also, some of these animals have evolved in chemically stable, pristine waters, and may thus be ultra sensitive to environmental changes. In general, aquatic animals do little in the way of internal detoxification of their waste

An aquarium (aquatic terrarium). Designed for exclusively aquatic species, this particular setup has an outside filter and drain.

products. In many cases, wastes with an extremely high ammonia content are released into the water. This functions well in the natural habitat, as the potentially lethal ammonia quickly dissipates in a large volume of water but in the aquarium, the animal's entire living medium can be rapidly poisoned. Filtration and, especially, partial and total water changes, thus become extremely important (see Filtration, page 39 for specifics). As a general rule, the largest volume of water that you can provide should be used. This acts as somewhat of a safety measure by allowing for some dilution of waste products but in no way replaces proper sanitation. Powerful filters can be used with some larger aquatic salamanders. The risk of an animal becoming stressed due to water currents created by these filters is not as great as with the newts, especially if the salamander is provided with a sheltered retreat. Some, such as the three species of giant salamander, family Cryptobranchidae, originate in flowing water and require high oxygen levels, which can be achieved through strong filtration if they are to thrive in captivity. A well-established undergravel filter is a tremendous asset to maintaining large aquatic specimens as the ammonia from waste products is rendered harmless by the activity of beneficial, aerobic bacteria; however, an undergravel filter requires a gravel bed. Many aquatic salamanders feed by powerful inhalations that inadvertently suck substrate into the mouth. Gravel impaction has been known to cause the death of Mexican axolotls, *Ambystoma mexicanum*. One way to avoid this is to use rocks that are too large to be swallowed, but the spaces between such rocks allow food animals to escape, and makes removal of dead food and solid waste products difficult.

In general, I have found that large aquatic specimens are best kept on bare bottoms with a powerful mechanical filter and with frequent partial or total water changes. Specimens that are habituated to feeding from tongs can be kept with an undergravel filter, as there is less of a chance of food animals escaping and dying below the rocks. A useful technique for maintaining an aquarium housing animals that need frequent cleaning is to have a plugged drain hole cut into the bottom of the tank. A hose can be attached by silicone to lead the water into a floor drain and screen placed over the hole if gravel is used.

Trout-holding Tanks

A very serviceable enclosure can be made for even the largest salamanders by using commercially available trout-holding tanks. These come in a variety of sizes. The largest can accommodate a breeding pair of Chinese or Japanese giant salamanders. They are equipped with chillers and powerful filters, so that even the most demanding cool water species can be accommodated. Submersible heaters can be installed, if necessary.

A larval peninsula newt, Notophthalmus viridescens piaropicola, *in a nicely decorated aquarium.*

Keeping Salamander Larvae

Keeping salamander larvae in an aquarium poses a different set of problems. While a large water volume is generally desirable (to promote normal growth and dilute waste products), salamander larvae need to eat a great deal, and generally do best when literally surrounded by food. In a large tank they do not seem particularly adept at locating food, and may fail to thrive. There are no hard-and-fast rules here, so these contradictory requirements will probably seem totally daunting to the less experienced hobbyist. However, patient observation will reveal the right balance between space and food availability.

The larvae must be able to avoid each other, as all appear to be cannibalistic. Filling the tank with artificial or real plants, especially those with lots of feathery branches, will help somewhat.

Water flow is critical here as most are weak swimmers. Also, larvae are easily sucked into filter intakes. Filter power can be cut by adding plastic sleeves over the intake. Other useful techniques are the use of undergravel filters or sponge filters, commercially marketed as "baby saver filters."

Young salamanders eat constantly, so water changes are the surest way of avoiding losses due to ammonia toxicity. Also, as with fish, a buildup of waste products, combined with crowding, may lead to abnormally slow growth or stunting of the larvae.

Subterranean and Cave Terrariums

Some of the most fascinating of all salamanders rarely if ever see the light of day, living as they do in underground streams, caves, or wells. It is likely that there are many still undiscovered species in such secret places. One turned up in Yugoslavia recently, in a cave that appears to have little or no connection to the outside world. There are indeed great strides to be

Bolitoglossa *species inhabit the rainforests of Mexico, Central America, and South America.*

made in the husbandry of these rare and little studied creatures; however, species such as the olm, *Proteus anguinus*, the Texas blind salamander, *Typhlomolge rathbuni*, and the Tennessee cave salamander, *Gyrinophilus palleucus*, are generally not available as captive-bred specimens, and are protected by law from collection. Should legal captive specimens become available, a trout-holding tank, modified to provide proper water flow and with subdued lighting, would seem a good enclosure with which to start. As these animals have evolved in an isolated situation, in what must be a very unique and stable set of environmental conditions, careful study of the natural environment (water quality, etc.) would be an absolute prerequisite for success with captives. Animals from such situations are notoriously sensitive to environmental changes, and are best studied by professionals.

A tropical terrarium. The pond (with an underground filter modified to operate in low water levels) helps maintain the high humidity required by tropical forest species.

Many arboreal species may be reluctant to descend to the ground and use a waterbowl; therefore, great care must be taken that their retreats contain enough moisture. Wet moss stuffed into arboreal caves, and live or plastic plants containing a small pool of water at their base will serve well in this regard. Certain orchids and bromiliads that can be cultured in the terrarium will hold small reserves of water that may be used by arboreal salamanders.

Outdoor Terrariums

Some of my fondest memories and most interesting observations center around a large outdoor terrarium I constructed. It housed mainly frogs and turtles—many salamanders are a bit harder to observe under outdoor conditions because of their secretive natures and moisture requirements. Nevertheless, large outdoor terrariums have great potential, especially in the area of captive breeding, as exposure to a natural seasonal cycle is usually necessary, as is the extra space offered by larger cages. The enclosure can be constructed of any of a variety of weatherproof materials. It is important to sink a screen or other barrier into the ground and to have it curve inward, to keep burrowing salamanders in and predators out. A sturdy cover is necessary, especially where animals such as raccoons are present. A shaded location should be chosen— morning sun may be okay as long as the inhabitants are able to remain cool and moist by burrowing beneath wet leaves, logs, or earth.

The range of behaviors that you can observe in an outdoor enclosure will usually far exceed those that take place in a more limited indoor setup. The problem is that since the salamanders have so much room, they will behave "naturally," which means you won't see much of them, especially

Tropical Forest Terrariums

While frogs and caecilians exhibit their greatest diversity in tropical forests, salamanders are poorly represented. Their greatest species diversity occurs in the cooler climate of the northeastern United States. A tropical forest terrarium can be fashioned following the general guidelines for the woodland terrarium. In the rain forest setup, a great amount of moisture is needed. Sphagnum moss is a good choice as a substrate because of its water-retaining properties. A water area in the terrarium is also a good idea. Most species from rain forests (chief among them are those of the genus *Bolitoglossa*, of Mexico and Central and South America) are terrestrial or arboreal, but a pool will help keep humidity high, especially if a submersible pump is used to create a small waterfall. A daily spraying is also beneficial. These methods are preferable to using a glass cover to raise humidity; despite the requirements for moist air, fresh air is also necessary.

during the day. Depending on your interest and finances, there are ways around this. There are lights available that are undetectable by most nocturnal animals but that allow humans to see. Night vision glasses may also be an option, and indirect yard lighting may be arranged so that you can observe the animals going about their usual activities undisturbed.

Wood and dead leaves will attract isopods, millipedes, and insects, as will small amounts of fruit or meat placed in the enclosure. Provided careful attention is paid to your captive's physical appearance in terms of weight, you may find that you'll need to provide little if any additional food. Watching salamanders feed on wild prey under seminatural conditions is a rare treat and a valuable learning experience.

Outdoor enclosures for large aquatic specimens offer a limitless range of possibilities—even swimming pools can be used. My experience with a tremendous array of captive animals has led me to believe that space, and access to natural light cycles and dietary variety (all of which are easier to provide, in some areas, outdoors) are critical elements that may allow us to maintain and breed a wider variety of species.

Mixed Species Enclosures

The mixed species terrarium presents a variety of problems that do not arise when we seek to keep animals in single species groups. A general rule with any group of animals is that it is unwise to mix closely related animals from different parts of the world. The microorganisms that dwell harmlessly inside a salamander from Japan, for example, may be able to thrive in a salamander from California (because of the general relatedness of the two species) but may cause health problems or death in the new host.

An outdoor terrarium. Note the underground screen to keep burrowers in and predators out.

Results of stress: Another possible problem is that of skin toxicity. I have no direct evidence concerning salamanders, but based on my experience with frogs and toads, it is possible that toxins released by some salamanders under stressful circumstances may kill others. For example, I've kept green frogs, *Rana clamitans*, and American toads, *Bufo americanus*, together in large terrariums for years with no problems. However, I know of someone who used a plastic bucket to transport toads and later, after the toads were removed, placed a green frog in the bucket. The frog promptly died, and an autopsy revealed that it had been poisoned, most likely by toxins that the toads had released upon being placed in a stressful situation (the bucket). So, err on the side of caution and, if you do attempt a mixed species exhibit, be sure the animals are not stressed. This can only be determined by careful observation of the animals during their normal activity periods. During the day, they may

Recently hatched albino axolotls, Ambystoma mexicanum, *are nearly transparent.*

in a large outdoor enclosure, thinking they will never cross paths. An example might be terrestrial *Ambystomids* (the tiger salamander, *Ambystoma tigrinum*) being kept in the land area and a greater siren, *Siren lacertina*, living in a large pool within the enclosure. But, most land-dwelling salamanders may enter water (or will fall in) during their nocturnal wanderings or when breeding, and most large aquatic salamanders will attempt to swallow any suitably sized animal they can catch. This could conceivably result in the loss of two animals, since skin toxins from the consumed creature could kill the predator.

Maintaining Large Colonies

When keeping large groups of salamanders for study purposes, or when raising young, ease of maintenance becomes a major consideration. For aquatic species, bare-bottom containers (plastic sweater boxes are ideal for many species) are recommended. The easiest shelters to use in this situation are plastic plants. These can be weighted down by adding a small stone, if necessary. I once came across some large plastic boxes with handles at a store close-out sale. Originally used as display boxes for clothes, they proved very useful for breeding aquatic species. If your circumstances permit, a quick way to service a large number of aquariums is to have drain holes drilled into the bottom of the tanks. Ideally, water would drain into a channel system or onto a concrete floor, where it would flow into a floor drain. Plastic children's pools can serve as inexpensive containers for large groups of larvae, but are hard to siphon if placed on the ground. Water changes can be made, however, using 5-gallon (19 L) buckets, and a variety of filters can be modified to fit these enclosures.

hide and all will appear to be well. Of course, severe stress will lead to obvious abnormalities, such as an animal wandering about restlessly at an inappropriate time, or one not seeking shelter when it should.

Keeping Similarly Sized Species Together

Your greatest chance for success will most likely be in keeping similarly sized species from the same geographic location or in keeping a terrestrial species with a similarly sized aquatic species from the same area. As an example of the first situation, I have maintained slimy salamanders, *Plethodon glutinosus*, with spotted salamanders, *Ambstoma maculatum*, and marbled salamanders, *Ambystoma opacum*. To illustrate the second situation, I have successfully kept red-backed salamanders, *Plethodon cinereus*, with the eastern newt, *Notopthalmus viridescens*. It may seem tempting to keep salamanders from vastly different habitats together

Plants for the Terrarium

Live Versus Artificial Plants

Live plants and artificial plants each have advantages and disadvantages, depending upon, among other things, the nature of your collection and the purposes for which you need plants. In addition to their aesthetic values, plants can fulfill a variety of practical functions in the terrarium. Live plants may serve the important role of natural soil and water filters, helping to keep the enclosure clean by using the waste products of the inhabitants. They also, of course, remove carbon dioxide and add oxygen to both water and air, benefiting the salamanders in the process and encouraging the growth of beneficial bacteria, which itself assists in the breakdown of nitrogenous waste products. Their production of oxygen prevents the establishment of anaerobic bacteria, which have been implicated in a variety of amphibian health problems. Live plants also provide shelter for terrarium inhabitants, and, if arranged properly, will reduce the light levels that reach the terrarium floor. This will keep temperatures lower and prevent an overly bright environment (most salamanders are more comfortable in subdued lighting). Plants can be arranged to function as sight barriers, and to give the animals a way to avoid each other. In an aquatic situation, dense plantings are among the best ways to prevent adults from eating larvae, and larvae from eating each other. Plant roots also help prevent areas of soil impaction.

Artificial plants are currently available in a great variety of very realistic models, and are manufactured from a variety of different materials, including plastic and silk. Plastic plants are suitable for all applications; silk plants should be used only in terrestrial installations. Artificial plants remove light as a consideration, since most salamanders do not require much in the way of supplementary lighting. They are easily sterilized and can be manipulated so as to construct breeding shelters, hideaways, etc. Those with many fine, branching leaves can be joined together and weighted down with a rock to provide shelters for larvae, and thus reduce cannibalism. Many are made so well that they are virtually indistinguishable from the real thing, especially when set up in a terrarium with real rocks, wood, and sphagnum moss. A live plant or two interspersed among the artificial does alot to hide their identity.

Important note: Do not use artificial plants with internal wire supports in aquatic situations. The wire will rust and possibly kill your salamanders. Since the existence of the wire will not be visible externally, you need to bend the plant to determine if the silk or plastic is molded over wire.

Useful Plant Species

Devil's Ivy *(Epipremnum aureum)*

Native to the Solomon Islands, this plant is, in my opinion, the most useful to the amphibian keeper. It can grow into an enormous vine with leaves nearly 1 foot (30 cm) across, but is easily managed in a terrarium through clipping. It will grow with only sphag-

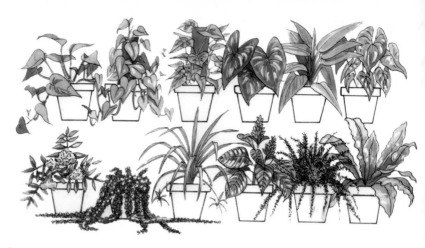

Plants for the terrarium. (From left to right, top row): devil's ivy, philodendron, satin pothos, arrowhead vine, Chinese evergreen, hooked strap plant; (bottom row): miniature wax plant, dwarf columnea, spider plant, zebra plant, asparagus fern, bird's nest fern.

num as a medium, and thrives in water for years. By clipping the leaves, the terrarist can "create" vines or other desirable forms. If rooted in shallow water, it takes the form of an emergent plant, and thus looks well in a bog terrarium. Devil's ivy can be removed when cleaning the tank and replaced with little fuss. Simply push the roots into sphagnum or just lay it on the surface. This amazing plant is nearly indestructible. When draped over logs and rocks, or when hanging, it sends out aereal roots that provide a great effect on both land and in water. Devil's ivy is tolerant of low light, will thrive in dry soil or in water, and re-grows from cuttings. The leaves vary greatly in appearance, each being streaked with a different pattern of cream and gold. When grown underwater, the stems and roots provide secure hiding places while still allowing the aquarium's inhabitants to be seen.

Other Recommended Houseplants

I have also found the following popular houseplants to be splendid additions to terrariums for newts and salamanders: heartleaf philodendron (*Philodendron scandens oxycardium*), satin pothos (*Scindapsus pictus*), arrowhead vine (*Syngonium podophyllum*), Chinese evergreen (*Aglaonema modestum*), miniature wax plant (*Hoya bella*), dwarf columnea (*Columnea microphylla*), spider plant (*Chlorophytum comosum variegatum*), zebra plant (*aphalandra squarrosa*), asparagus fern (*Asparagus densiflorus*), bird's nest fern (*Asplenium nidus*), miniature creeping fig (*Ficus pumila minima*), and hooked strap plant (*Anthurium hookeri*).

Tip: The coffee plant (*Coffa arabica*) can survive in surprisingly wet conditions, and is excellent as background foliage. It does well in medium light, but requires bright light to flower.

The Terrarium's Physical Parameters

pH Levels

pH is the level of acidity or alkalinity of water. On the pH scale, which runs from 0 to 14, 7 is considered neutral, but, actually, a neutral reading is very rare in nature. Each particular species of salamander (and many other animals) has an adaptation to a specific pH level. While there are many exceptions, in general, amphibians are sensitive to water that is too acidic and also too alkaline, although acidity seems to be more of a problem in most captive environments. I have found that most salamanders do well at a pH of 7 or as close to that as possible—in other words, at 6.5 to 7.5. Ideally, one should take pH readings of both water and land in the natural habitat in which the particular salamanders originated. Soil pH also affects terrestrial salamanders, and many have been disappearing from areas where the soil has become acidic due to the influence of acid rain. A range of 6.5 to 7.5 will work well for most species except those that are specifically adapted to higher or lower pH levels, for example cave-dwelling salamanders or those that live in creeks running over limestone. These animals would more likely be adapted to a very alkaline environment. There are a variety of commercially available test kits that are simple to operate and that instantly measure pH levels of water. pH strips, which are generally available through medical suppliers, are also very easy to use and provide instant readings. The pH of water, both in the natural and captive environment, changes over time. Waste products, uneaten food, and decaying plants in the aquarium will all lead to an acidic condition. Most amphibians are stressed at levels below 6, and many die at a pH of 5.5 or below. In years past I have often wondered about the lack of salamanders and frogs in what appeared to be an ideal habitat within certain pine barren ponds and streams on Long Island, New York. Upon measuring the pH of the water, I found it to be generally around 5.5, which could explain the absence of these creatures. There are, at least among the frogs, species that are especially adapted to highly acidic conditions. Less is known about salamanders possessing such adaptations.

Tip: If an animal is experiencing stress from acidic conditions in your aquarium, it can sometimes be rescued by placing it in cool, clean water. I prefer to use bottled spring water. Do not use distilled water and do not make the water too deep, especially if the animal is in a weakened condition. I use just enough water to barely cover the salamander. This will often serve to flush the animal's system and prevent the illness or death that can result from being confined to an acidic environment for too long.

Signs of pH Stress

Animals suffering pH stress will at first appear restless and move about on the surface or in areas they do not usually frequent and at times when

pH strips are easy to use and provide instant readings.

If a normally secretive bottom-dwelling lesser siren, Siren intermedia, *swims rapidly on the surface of the tank, this may indicate a water quality problem.*

they are not usually active. They will become lethargic and appear to lack muscle tone when picked up.

Making pH Changes

In general, the rule is to make pH changes slowly. If you are moving a newly purchased animal to a new environment or new water, for example, slowly mix both the new and the old water. Rapid pH changes of two points or more kill most fish and although specific information is lacking for salamanders, that might be a general rule to follow. Those salamanders from stable environments where little change takes place naturally in the course of a year, such as caves or wells, would be far more sensitive to pH changes. Therefore, any changes should be made very gradually and one should attempt to provide the exact pH levels in captivity that the animal is adapted to in the wild. What we have said concerning pH applies to land as well. Waste products and uneaten food in the substrate of a terrestrial tank will also change the pH.

The land-dwelling salamander absorbing water through its skin will be affected by the acidic condition of the soil or moss in much the same way as an aquatic species. Red-backed salamanders have been shown to become stressed at soil pH levels below 6 and will try to leave the area. If prevented from doing so, and if confined to such a pH, they eventually die.

Tip: Although acidic conditions are generally to be avoided in captivity, note that ammonia is more toxic at an alkaline pH than it is at an acidic pH. For example, the same amount of ammonia dissolved in water at pH 7.8 would be more dangerous to the animals than at pH 6.8.

Type of Water

Because of the widespread problem of acid rain, collecting rainwater is often no longer an option as a way of providing pure water for your captives. Distilled water is also to be avoided as it can draw out certain ions and salts from the salamander's body. The best choice is usually commercially available bottled spring water (such as that marketed by Deer Park, Poland Spring, etc.). There are a variety of chemicals available that will adjust your aquarium's water to a specific pH level. These products, sold by the tropical fish trade, are available for pH levels of 6.5, 7, and 7.5.

Tip: Additives cannot maintain pH levels, and the pH will change as conditions in the aquarium or terrarium change—such as the addition of waste products, uneaten food, or decaying plant material.

Water Hardness and Softness

Water hardness is a measurement of the dissolved calcium and magnesium. One degree of hardness equals one part per million (ppm) of calcium carbonate in water. While there are no specific levels that indicate "hard" or soft," 0 to 50 degrees may be considered soft water; 50 to 100 degrees, moderately hard; 100 degrees, hard; and 200, very hard. As a general rule please note this is *very* general), most fish do well in moderately hard water, that is, 100 degrees of hardness or 100 ppm. Little work has been done concerning the effects of water hardness on salamanders in either wild or captive situations. Test kits are available from tropical fish product suppliers to measure hardness. As with pH, hardness in the wild varies throughout the year. At low water levels, calcium and magnesium in the water is concentrated and hardness increases. During rains or flood periods, more water is added, the minerals are diluted, and the water becomes softer. Rapid changes in hardness have been shown to spur certain fish into breeding. Since many salamanders breed after the spring rains, when the water levels are rising and the water hardness decreases, it is possible that this would, in general, be a breeding cue for captive salamanders as well. Animals living in deep wells, caves, or streams that flow over limestone would be adapted to hard water conditions as these situations result in water high in calcium. Those species from still water swamps and other areas with muddy bottoms would, in general, be adapted to soft water.

Tip: Gravel, rocks, and other materials that are added to the aquarium can influence the hardness of the water and in such a limited water volume situation might cause a problem. Again, the parameters are not really known as much less has been done in this area than, for example, in the area of pH levels.

Ammonia

Ammonia is a poisonous intermediate by-product of the breakdown of organic material by bacteria. It is also excreted by salamanders as part of their waste products. Salamanders and amphibians, in general, as well as fish, are extremely sensitive to ammonia levels, both in the water and on land. Since ammonia is colorless and odorless and *extremely* lethal, it presents a particularly difficult problem in captive maintenance of amphibians. It is the probable cause of many deaths of captive animals. It can literally kill an animal in several hours and is especially troublesome in crowded conditions or with large specimens. Also, highly aquatic animals release more ammonia with their waste products than do terrestrial species. Aquatic frogs, for example, excrete nearly pure ammonia. Since the ammonia dissolves rapidly and spreads throughout the water and land areas, the creatures therein have no way to escape it and will succumb rapidly. Salamanders stressed by ammonia levels will exhibit some of the same reactions as were discussed under pH. They become restless and active at unusual times, and thereafter become lethargic and appear flaccid when picked up. As with pH stress, confinement in shallow, cool spring water will help to flush the ammonia from the animal's system. Septicemia or red leg (see page 60) is often associated with conditions of high ammonia buildup. In addition to its introduction by the animal's waste products, overfeeding, and the presence of dead animals, food animals, and dying plants will all add to the ammonia level. Also, decorative items placed into the tank, such as logs and rocks, may contain within them dead plant and animal material that will raise ammonia levels. Beware of using fertilizers on live plants.

Tip: If the plant is not able to survive on whatever waste products are produced by the animals in the tank, it should be fertilized outside of the tank and given time to absorb the material added.

Bottled water is often the best choice for your specimens.

Removing Ammonia

The most effective way of removing ammonia from a system is to follow strict cleaning protocol. Water changes work best. Please note that adding water to replace evaporated water does not remove ammonia; the fresh water will help dilute the ammonia remaining in the tank, but water changes are really the only way to get the ammonia out. Undergravel filters, if properly established, do an excellent job of detoxifying ammonia. Nitrifying bacteria living on the gravel break down organic wastes to nitrates, which are deadly, and finally to nitrites, which are harmless to the aquarium's inhabitants. Outside filters will also support a growth of aerobic or nitrifying bacteria, but not to the levels that the gravel bed will. Since the nitrifying bacteria are aerobic and require oxygen to survive, your aquarium pump should always be running. It has been said that as little as 15 minutes with no oxygen can kill off large portions of the nitrifying bacteria population, although I have not noticed this in my experience. A product called Ammo-chips, which can be placed into outside filters, is said to remove ammonia from the water. However, its effectiveness is limited—the chips become saturated and ineffective, but do not give any indication of when this has occurred. Follow the instructions on the box regarding the amount to put in for the size of the tank you have. Gravel cleaners, which are used to remove suspended material from within the gravel bed, do no harm to the nitrifying bacteria.

Copper

Copper is a medication, but at certain levels may be toxic to a variety of amphibians. Copper pipes, especially in very old buildings, will leach copper into the water, but at varying levels throughout the day. In the morning, if the water has not been used all night, copper levels will be very high—high enough to kill even such hardy amphibians as the African clawed frog, *Xenopus laevis*. After running for about an hour, depending upon the size of the water system in question, copper levels will fall. A test kit should be used to check the water from your supply at various times during the day to determine if and when copper is present.

Chlorine, Chloramine, and Other Additives to Tap Water

Chlorine and chloramine are added to tap water for health reasons, but pass through the skin of salamanders and cause sickness or death, both through internal effects on the animal and the actual contact with the sensitive skin. I always make it a practice to dechlorinate all water used for captive amphibians. A commercially available product, Wardley's Chlor-Out, has proven very effective and works instantly. If chloramine is present in your water, be sure to use a product that detoxifies chloramine as well as chlorine. A call to your local water authority is necessary to determine what chemicals are added to your tap water. Water can also be dechlorinated by allowing it to stand for 24 hours in an open container. This process can be hastened by the addition of an air stone to the water. For rare species, or those from extremely stable environments, or in many cases for the larvae of aquatic species, bottled water is a safe alternative. Be sure to not use distilled water and to test various brands to determine their suitability for the species in which you are interested.

Pond and Rainwater

As mentioned previously, rainwater needs to be tested to determine its acidity before being used in the terrarium. There also may be other compounds or chemicals in rainwater that are not detectable through the available test kits, so one would probably be safer, unfortunately, to avoid rainwater. Pond water might be an alternative, especially if there are healthy populations of amphibians living in the water you choose to use. Be aware that the fact that amphibians are there does not necessarily mean that the water is safe. The population may be in trouble and various parasites and predators can be introduced through the use of pond water. Many of these creatures in the larval stage are tiny and might not be noticed until they begin to grow and cause problems. Note also that the pH and chemistry of pond water will change within the aquarium. Certain animals that might be introduced into the aquarium, such as snails, are intermediate hosts for a variety of parasites that affect captive animals. Wild animals might have specific immunities that are lacking in captive-bred specimens. Also, in the wild animals are killed by parasites, a situation that we are looking to avoid in captivity. One use of pond water is to provide food for the tiny larvae. Generally, however, this is not as important as it is in raising certain filter feeding species of frog tadpoles. Most salamander larvae, even the tiniest, will take newly hatched brine shrimp or chopped blackworms.

Humidity

Generally, salamanders require high humidity and small microhabitats within the terrarium where it is very damp. A pool, especially if it is in contact with the substrate, can provide this and humidity can be increased by covering the screen top directly over the pool with glass or plastic. Covering the entire top will greatly increase humidity but cut down too much on the ventilation. A rain system might be installed. These are available commercially or can be created with a large sprayer set in the "On" position for a varying length of time. Commercially available sprayers usually used to spray insecticide and that hold about 2 gallons (7 L) of water are ideal. Be aware that a drainage system needs to be set up in the bottom of the terrarium so that water does not merely pool up inside.

Gravel reserve: An extremely effective way of maintaining dampness and high humidity is to have a gravel reserve—a gravel layer below the moss or soil in the terrarium. Water trapped within the gravel gradually leaches into the moss and maintains moisture. This also seems to keep sphagnum and carpet moss in better shape than just laying it on the bottom of the tank and wetting it. Periodic cleaning is essential, however, as the water within the gravel will become stagnant rapidly. For large tanks, which cannot be dumped and rinsed, a drainage hole should be cut in the bottom, which can be plugged and unplugged as needed.

Home heating, especially forced air heating, will rapidly dry out tanks, so be sure to check this.

Pools: For highly terrestrial species, a pool might still be provided for emergencies, but be sure that the animals can easily enter and exit the water area. Wet sphagnum in a small cave will serve as a place to go should the tank dry out unexpectedly. Tanks set up within a larger enclosure that has water on the bottom, such as the Living Stream system described on page 49, might also be a useful situation, especially for times when the humidity cannot be monitored daily.

Filtration

The Undergravel Filter

One of the most effective filters is the undergravel filter. Beware, of course, of the size of the gravel used,

An undergravel filter. Water is drawn through the gravel, nourishing the essential aerobic bacteria.

Starter cultures for the aerobic bacteria might be obtained from gravel in a well-established tank, or by keeping a single animal in the tank for a time, or by purchasing the bacteria at a pet store specializing in tropical fish. This last option is quite a shock for us "old-timers." I have had a good deal of success with such commercially available aerobic bacteria.

Gravel washers: Note that large particles are not removed by the undergravel filter and are sucked into the gravel bed; therefore, a gravel washer or a finely meshed net should be used to remove them. Ideally, the net might be used after feeding and a gravel washer used on a regular basis to remove suspended particles. A gravel washer is a siphon tube that sucks gravel partially up its length and clears it of particulate matter trapped in the gravel bed. Even though the suspended material may be chemically harmless, it will cloud the water eventually if it is not removed. An alternative technique is to use a mechanical filter in addition to an undergravel filter (see page 41), but even in such a setup periodic gravel washing is necessary. Of course, the tank can be dismantled and the gravel rinsed, but this may disrupt the bacterial colonies, and for a large aquarium it would be virtually impossible. An undergravel filter might be the only viable method, aside from a bare-bottom tank.

so that the animals cannot swallow the stones. The operation of the filter is such that water is drawn down through the gravel and returned up through plastic tubes, nourishing aerobic bacteria in the process and inhibiting the growth of harmful anaerobic bacteria. The return tubes can be cut so that any size pool or tank with any depth of water can be filtered, even a small pool in a terrestrial setup (see page 38 for a more detailed explanation of the working of the undergravel filter). A powerhead added directly to the return tube is a way of increasing the filtration power of the undergravel filter. These are also marketed in a variety of small sizes and shapes. Water is returned straight up so that strong currents are not established in the tank. Undergravel filters are especially good for larvae and smaller creatures because they do not suck in the animals or the food items as might a powerful outside or corner filter.

Regular Water Changes

The use of an undergravel filter, or any type of filtration for that matter, does not do away with the need for regular water changes. Even in a highly efficient system with both undergravel and mechanical filtration, ammonia can and will build up and should be removed periodically through a 20 to 30 percent water change every week, two weeks, or a month, depending on the population of salamanders and the size of the aquarium. The best way to determine how often to do water changes is to purchase an ammonia test kit from your local pet store. These are relatively inexpensive and easy to operate. Most work on a color system where one compares the color of a sample after an agent is added with a color chart to determine the approximate ammonia level in the tank. This is accurate enough for our purposes. Once ammonia levels are established, one can easily decide on a schedule of water changes that will keep the levels in check. Also, the periodic changes will prevent the yellowing of the water that occurs with aging.

Types of Filters

In addition to undergravel filters, there are a variety of other models available for use with salamanders.

Small inside, corner filters operated by external air pumps, while unsightly, are quite effective if the airflow to them is sufficiently powerful. In addition to mechanical removal of the detritus in the water, bacteria will grow on the filtering substrate (usually activated carbon and cotton) and assist in chemically breaking down the waste products therein. The filter should be left on at all times so as to insure a constant supply of oxygen for the aerobic or beneficial bacteria.

When replacing the filter medium, one should always add a bit of old filter medium to the new batch. This will introduce helpful bacteria, which will quickly repopulate the new filter substrate. One must be particularly careful that larvae or small food items are not sucked into the filter. Ideally, a corner filter should have low and high intake holes so that dirty water will be sucked from the very bottom of the tank as well as at a level slightly above this. As with the undergravel filter, the outflow of water is directed upwards so that potentially harmful currents are not established.

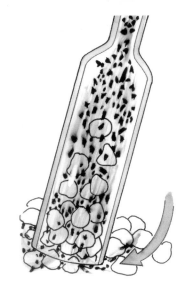

A gravel washer will remove particles that become lodged in the gravel bed.

Sponge filters: The ideal inside filter for tiny larvae or delicate specimens is the sponge filter, usually marketed as a "baby saver" in pet stores as it was originally designed for use with baby tropical fish. Water is effectively filtered and particles mechanically removed, yet small delicate creatures are not sucked into a motor or filter. The filter is cleaned merely by running cool water through it. I would not use hot water, (except when it is being sterilized), because this would kill the beneficial bacteria that will grow on the sponge and that assist in rendering the waste products therein chemically harmless.

Other inside filters: More recently, inside filters where the motor and the filtration unit are within a single submersible container, have been introduced into the pet trade. These can be operated in fairly low water and are available in a variety of sizes. Their chief limitation, in my opinion, is that they generally do not allow for a large amount of carbon and Ammo-chips to be introduced into the system. Basically they function by drawing water through a small cylindrical filter pad. Sometimes this is impregnated with carbon but not really enough to do any amount of good in terms of water clarity. They can do an effective job of mechanically cleaning the water, however, and bacteria will develop on the surface within so that some biological filtration will occur. They produce very rapid currents that are best diverted toward the surface. They also generally draw water through a very small area. Their use is pretty much limited to small pond sections in large terrariums or to bare-bottom tanks that are also given thorough cleanings and water changes on a regular basis.

Rain system: One model has an adaptation that allows for the creation of a waterfall system. This can also be modified to create a rain system through a series of tubes. The rain system is invaluable for breeding for a variety of frogs and most likely it

Make certain that small, delicate specimens can't be trapped by the filter apparatus.

would be useful with many salamanders as well.

Outside filters, those that hang outside the aquarium and have tubes that extend into the water section, are generally usable only for fully aquatic specimens and present some limitations. Older models will not operate unless the aquarium is nearly filled with water, although the newer ones will draw water from a shallow area and return it in a sort of waterfall system. The siphon tubes can usually be easily dislodged by powerful aquatic animals and, once the suction is lost, filtration stops. Also, since there are generally large tubes extending into the tank, it is extremely difficult to create an escape-proof environment. At night many aquatic specimens will wander and push about at the surface of the tank and find any exit hole. The entrance hole for the filtration tubes provides such an opportunity and indeed, the tubes themselves may be used, for example, the animal might swim up the tube into the filter box and then onto the floor.

Canister filters: More effective are canister filters, which are large filters with powerful motors, generally mounted on the floor below the aquarium. The tubes entering and leaving are flexible and can be fitted into small holes cut into the tank top. They are very hard, if not impossible, to dislodge so that constant filtration is ensured. Also, the motors are usually far more powerful than those available with hanging outside filters, so better filtration is ensured for large specimens. Several will operate at very low water levels and they also can be used, much like the submersible motors, for the creation of waterfalls and/or rain systems.

Commercial Preparations to Alter Water Chemistry

A variety of liquid chemicals are available to change or influence water

An inside corner filter. Activated charcoal and cotton (or synthetic floss) remove detritus from the water; aerobic bacteria help break down waste products.

quality. In the old days, substances such as peat moss and baking soda were used to increase or decrease pH levels. Today, one can purchase products that will set the pH to a desired level. Of course checking with chemical test kits is still necessary. There are also products that will, it is said, maintain pH for a long period of time, but I am not familiar with their use. One useful chemical product is the dechlorinator and there are other products that remove chloromine from the water (see page 38).

There are also liquids that are said to help replace the slim coat of fish, especially of those that have been stressed during capture or shipment. Aloe vera is usually the active ingredient. Most of these will also remove chlorine and chloramine. One such product is StressCoat, which I have used with some success on frogs and salamanders. Also developed for the fish trade are products that leach out heavy metals and minerals from the water. (Elements such as copper can be detrimental to fish and certainly to amphibians.) There are also many sophisticated units that can be attached to a water supply and that remove a variety of minerals from the water. I would steer away from those products that claim to "instantly" clear up the water because, if the water in your tank is foul and cloudy, there is a reason and masking that condition without correcting it will lead to the death of your specimens. Water clarity is not necessarily an indication that the water is chemically safe. Uneaten food and feces will foul the water, turn it chemically unsuitable for your animals, and will kill them even while the water appears clear. In this regard, one should note that ammonia is virtually colorless and odorless except at high concentrations. Since most of the aquatic salamanders' waste products are in the form of liquid, one cannot go

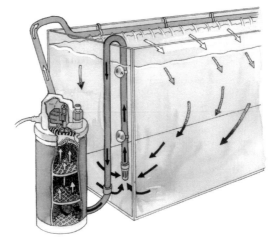

A canister filter. Canisters, which are usually quite powerful, may be placed beneath or beside the tank.

by water appearance in determining when to clean an animal's enclosure.

Lighting

In recent years a great deal of work has been done in connection with the lighting requirements of reptiles. It has been discovered that a variety of reptiles require full-spectrum light or, more specifically, light within a certain wavelength, in order to synthesize vitamin D and thereby utilize dietary calcium. This has not been greatly studied in amphibians, except in connection with the disappearance of certain species. It seems that ultraviolet light is reaching the earth in possibly higher concentrations in some areas, perhaps due to a thinning of the ozone layer. This has been linked to amphibian disappearances, especially among montane species. It has been found that salamander eggs that are laid in the open water where sunlight would hit them generally have a natural UV protectant. Those that lay in protected areas, such as under stumps and rocks, do not have this protection. Therefore, it would follow that at least certain concentrations of ultraviolet light are harmful to some amphibian eggs and possibly larvae. This should be kept in mind when incubating eggs. Animals that lay in protected areas should be allowed to do so and their eggs, if removed from the laying site, should not be incubated under bright light of any kind, especially full-spectrum light. Since most adult salamanders do not, in the natural state, experience long-term exposure to ultraviolet light, I would not think that it would be necessary for them in captivity. Terrestrial species are rarely out in the daytime and if they are it is under circumstances where they are generally not exposed to direct sunlight. So again, I don't think there is a need for exposure to UV light. A fluorescent light or a light specifically designed for plant growth will probably do no harm if the salamanders are able to avoid it. In fact, maintaining a proper light cycle even though the salamanders are hiding

during the day is important in order to induce breeding. Of course, plant growth will not take place without proper light and this is a consideration if you are keeping living plants with salamanders. If the salamanders are not being maintained with live plants, room lighting can be used. A window that lets in a normal daylight cycle would also be useful. Fluorescent light does not give off much in the way of heat, so except in a very small tank there is little fear in that regard. Incandescent light generally has no purpose in salamander maintenance because of the large amount of heat generated. A very small bulb might be used to create a day/night cycle, but even this would be more safely used in a lamp at some distance from the enclosure.

Manipulating the Physical Parameters to Induce Breeding

As you will see from a review of the various species accounts (beginning on page 71), the breeding cycle of most salamanders is strongly tied to seasonal climatic conditions. Reptiles and amphibians may live for years under optimal conditions but not reproduce unless the proper cycle of cold, rain, dry periods, humidity, water level increase and decrease, etc. are provided. Some of the equipment that we have previously discussed can be used to mimic a variety of seasonal changes and to help establish a salamander breeding program.

Rain Chamber

One technique that has been successfully used with a great many frog species is an artificial rain chamber. While there are commercial rain machines available on the market in sizes small enough to be used in a 20- to 50-gallon (76–189 L) aquarium, one can easily construct a simple chamber using a submersible pump

A rain chamber powered by a canister filter. You will have to research the natural climatic cycles of your specimens to determine when to turn the "rain" on and off.

or an outsider canister filter. In either case the return tubes from the filter are fastened to a screen top of the aquarium. Generally, extra return tubes will need to be purchased. They are linked together in several rows so that most of the screened area of the cover of the tank is traversed by the return tubes. Small holes are punched into the tubes and they are connected to the outflow of the canister filter or the submersible pump. Water from a pool area in the aquarium is sucked into the motor and returned into the tank as artificial rain. When to actually "turn the rain on" (time of day or night, season) is determined by researching climatic cycles of your specimens' natural habitat. An electric timer can then be used to imitate these cycles.

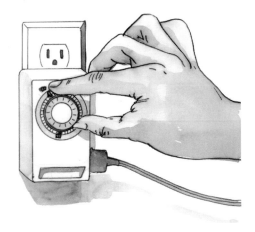

A simple electrical timer can be used to maintain the proper light cycle.

Light Cycles

Lighting is a little studied aspect in the general biology of salamanders, and although most are nocturnal creatures and spend the day hidden, I believe it is important to stimulate a normal seasonal light cycle. This can be easily done with a timer, matching the hours of lightness and darkness to those that occur in the animals' natural habitat. An alternative method, if you live within the range of the salamanders that you are trying to breed, is to have the aquarium or terrarium set in a location where it will experience a natural light cycle. I don't think the light intensity or directness of the rays is as important as the fact that the area is light for a proper amount of time and dark for a proper amount of time. Incidentally, a good meteorology book that discusses world climate will allow you to track what may be going on in the areas where the salamander originally lived. Be sure to check for isolated pockets or areas within the salamanders' range that might experience different overall weather patterns than the rest of the area. Factors such

as the location of mountain ranges, distance from the ocean, etc., may cause small areas within certain climatic belts to experience totally different weather patterns and this may of course affect the breeding biology of the population living within these areas.

Many terrestrial salamanders will need access to a large body of water in which to reproduce, and size of the body of water and water depth may affect their reproductive output. Most *ambystomids,* for example, spend their adult lives on land but return to a pond in which to lay eggs. These animals would need the simulation of rain plus the gradual warming of the soil as well as a suitably sized water area. In this regard, provide the largest container possible and be sure that the water is filled several inches deep and that the animals have easy access to and from the water area.

Stimulating Breeding

Actually placing gravid females and reproductively active males into a pond situation may be necessary for some terrestrial salamanders. The physical presence of the pond may then stimulate breeding, as appears to be the case for certain types of frogs. Temperature manipulation is another concern when seeking to reproduce salamanders in captivity. Some may not need a "winter" period of the length experienced in the wild; four to six weeks seems to work for many temperate species. In many cases, temperature need not be dropped as low as would occur in the natural situation. Terrestrial frogs such as wood frogs, *Rana sylvatica*, freeze solid in the winter during hibernation, protected from death by a form of natural glycogen. Many terrestrial salamanders seem to hibernate in areas where they might also experience something similar; however, in captivity it is safer and usually as effective to chill the animals below their normal active range but not to the temperatures they might experience in the wild. A refrigerator might prove very useful for this part of your operation. Unheated basements and attics can also be utilized, and there has been some success in the overwintering of certain species outdoors. Again, if you are using a refrigerator or an unheated room, be sure to take the temperatures at different times of the year and at different parts of the room to establish an overall pattern before placing your animals in them.

Changes in humidity are less well known in terms of their effect upon reproduction biology. I suspect that the gradual increase in rain and the change in temperature would be enough to satisfy any humidity increase or decrease that might be necessary. For certain newts such as the crested newt, *Triturus cristatus*, a mere increase in water volume is often enough to stimulate reproduction if the animals are in good condition. For example, crested newts kept in a 15-gallon (57 L) tank, may be suffi-

ciently stimulated by a move to a 55-gallon (208 L) tank with its increased water depth, to reproduce without prior conditioning such as hibernation.

General Cleaning Considerations

It has been mentioned before that water changes are the most effective way of ensuring a clean environment for your animals. Water changes can be partial or total. Of course a total water change places some stress on the animal if the water chemistry and/or temperature is very different from the water to which the animal has been accustomed. This can be easily checked and avoided. One thing to be particularly careful of is moving animals that have been kept in an improperly cleaned aquarium (or even a well-filtered one with no water changes) for a long period of time. The animal may gradually adjust to the worsening water conditions, such as rising ammonia levels and acidity. If partial water changes are not made, even if the aquarium is well filtered the water will take on a character of its own and become chemically very unique. This will make introduction of new animals extremely difficult and long-time inhabitants of the aquarium may experience a great deal of stress or even die when moved to an aquarium with better water quality, something I have seen many times among fish. In one case, an individual of a very hardy species, the southeast Asian snakehead, lived for two years in a large, well-filtered tank with barely any water changes being made. When the animal was eventually removed to a new, clean aquarium, it died overnight. The shock of the chemistry change was apparently too great for the fish even though the water to which it was moved was actually of far better quality than the water from which it had originated.

Introducing Objects into the Enclosure

Before discussing actually cleaning out aquariums and terrariums, I should mention that objects, natural or otherwise, introduced to the enclosure, such as logs, rocks, etc., should be carefully examined first for potential pests and also for dead or decomposing material within. The best way to approach this is to soak any new items in a chlorine solution overnight. They must of course be rinsed thoroughly after being submerged in chlorine. This is not usually a problem with rocks, although some very porous ones may take extra time. Perhaps a safer route would be to use common household salt. One-half cup per gallon of water would most likely be sufficient to render the objects safe for your use. Water chemistry can be affected by rocks that are introduced into the aquarium. Tried and proven rock such as shale or schist is safe. As for actually disinfecting, use hot water. Salt is an invaluable aid. Although it is not much in favor today, I have used it for many years with great success for cleaning enclosures and objects within the aquarium and terrarium. One useful aspect of salt is that it easily rinses away, so one need not worry as much about lingering residues as would be the case with commercial disinfectants.

Allowing enclosures, rocks, etc., to dry in the sun is ideal. Many of the pads sold for cleaning aquariums are quite useful for the salamander keeper. They do not scratch glass, yet are rough enough to remove any residue that might stick to the surfaces. Methyline blue is an excellent disinfectant not so much for cleaning purposes but for soaking aquariums that have housed sick animals. It is also a useful medicine. A drawback is that it stains hands and certain types of wood. In the concentration normally marketed for the tropical fish trade it is harmless to salamanders.

In considering water changes and their frequency, it must be remembered that moss, or whatever substrate you use, also needs to be cleaned or replaced at regular intervals. Waste and ammonia will build up within the substrate in the same manner as it will in water. While carpet moss can be rinsed once or twice, especially if it is a thick piece, and reused, it is best to replace this and the sphagnum moss when cleaning is required.

Cleaning is one of the most overlooked aspects of amphibian maintenance.

Commercial disinfectants are not generally necessary unless there is a disease problem or for some reason there is a particularly foul condition in an exhibit. Novolsan or microquat are powerful, commercially available disinfectants widely used by zoological parks but their use is not indicated for amphibians unless there is a particular problem as they linger and are extremely hard to rinse off many surfaces. I would not use them at all on wood, because they seep in and will slowly leach out even after long soakings. Both are lethal for all amphibians.

Bleach: If conditions are really bad and something stronger than household salt and hot water are indicated, I would use bleach. It is a powerful disinfectant and will most likely kill and clean whatever it is you are seeking to kill or clean and it rinses much more easily from surfaces so that traces are not left behind to poison your animals. It takes a surprisingly small amount of these chemicals to kill a salamander. Remember that salamanders take in alot of water and associated chemicals though their skin.

Freezing has been suggested as an alternative method to disinfect porous items such as logs and certain rock and, while I have not experimented with this, it would certainly bear looking into.

HOW-TO:
Temperature Control

Heating

Heat is rarely a problem in the captive maintenance of salamanders, since even tropical species generally find microhabitats within the ecosystem where they can regulate their temperatures to slightly cooler levels than are available in general. Heating might be necessary where one is trying to simulate a seasonal change outside of the local weather cycle. Water heaters designed for the tropical fish and reptile trade are adequate.

Submersible heaters are available that operate in as little as 2 inches (5 cm) of water, so they can even be used in a terrestrial terrarium with a small pond section. They will heat the air as well as the substrate with which the water is in contact. It helps to put plastic over the pond side of the screen cover in order to help retain heat, but beware of curtailing ventilation. An older method was to use a fish heater in a water-filled jar, but one must be careful that salamanders do not come in contact with the very hot glass or crawl into the water and cook. Also, water evaporates from the jar, and dry conditions damage or break the heater.

Heating a pond area is simpler and more effective. The variety of hot rocks and subsurface heating pads currently available are generally not suitable for salamanders as they heat just a specific spot and

Placing a terrarium near a basement window can be a simple and effective way to control temperature and light for certain species.

salamanders generally do not bask to warm up. Also, the area heated, such as the glass above the heat pad, tends to become too hot for most species.

Incandescent lighting as a heating source is generally not feasible as it results in too bright a condition within the

aquarium or terrarium and also dries the air and the substrate as well, a situation to be avoided.

Ceramic heaters, which give off heat but not light, are a slightly better choice; however, most are very strong, being designed for reptiles, and will also rapidly dry out a tank.

A submersible heater. Heating might be necessary when you are trying to simulate a seasonal change.

Other heaters: Perhaps the safest method to increase temperature is to use a space heater or an oil-filled radiator in the room in which the terrarium is located. This allows for an overall change of temperature without creating specific hot spots in the terrarium.

Cooling

Cooling is more often a consideration. The temperatures in the summertime in the normal home environment in the northeastern United States are often too warm for many species of salamanders. Thermometers placed at various areas within your home throughout the year will enable you to determine the temperature patterns. Temperature preferences will vary by species; in general, however 50° to 60°F (10–16°F) will be satisfactory. A basement is generally a better choice than the main living area of the home. If one is available to you, take temperatures there to determine its suitability. Most salamanders will live well in a darkened basement, but for breeding purposes terrariums should be located where they can receive a natural light cycle through the window, or a small bulb should be set up on a timer in the room.

Cold water lines run through the tank are a way to cool water and land, but are costly to install and waste a good deal

When cooling is necessary, several tanks can be located in a large refrigerated unit.

of water as they need to be running all the time.

Trout-storage tanks: An ideal setup for cooling animals is a commercially available trout-storage tank. One marketed as Living Stream is a large refrigerated unit that can be used for large aquatic species, community tanks of terrestrial animals, or, where a breeding pond is necessary, for large terrestrial species, such as tiger salamanders, *Ambystoma tigrinum*. Also, such units could be used to store smaller tanks; for example, the cool water running within a living stream might be used as a cooling system for a variety of small plastic enclosures kept within the stream.

Other cooling methods: Air conditioning a room to the proper temperature is another alterna-

tive, and, in emergencies, running tanks under cold water several times a day will bring down the temperature significantly. Unused refrigerators might prove ideal if the temperature settings can be arranged to accommodate the species in which you are interested and are also useful for hibernation areas, but you might want to run this idea by those you live with before replacing milk cartons with boxes of salamanders! Bob Holland, a friend who has had incredible success with a variety of delicate species, uses a cooler with ice packs in which to permanently house small enclosures for particularly delicate animals. Initial experimentation as to the size of the ice pack and length of time they retain their cooling properties is necessary.

Warnings: Electrical Hazards

It is very easy to get caught up in adding to and maintaining a collection and in the process to neglect proper caution in operating the electrical appliances associated with terrarium keeping. Be aware of the following points:

• Pumps, filters, chillers, lights, etc., cannot be indiscriminately added to one's circuitry.

• All warnings on each appliance *must* be read and adhered to. This particularly applies to pumps, which should be mounted as discussed in the directions, for example, generally higher than the tank and with a drip loop.

• It is very tempting and easy to add extension cords randomly as one's collections grows, but please read the rating for each cord and the rating of the equipment you plug into it and pay attention to your fuse or circuit box.

• I would definitely recommend that you call in a licensed electrician to look over your setup and make recommendations.

• If you have other pets that are free-roaming, be sure that they cannot upset any equipment that might cause a fire. Each year I hear stories of animals—such as dogs, cats, or rabbits—that were roaming around and managed to knock over a lamp that fell onto something flammable and burned down the house. If you keep other animals such as reptiles, also be aware that an escaped snake or large lizard can do an incredible amount of damage both in terms of turning things over and in causing fires.

• Be especially carefully of portable room heaters; not all are designed to operate continuously. Make sure the model you choose is fit for the purpose to which you put it, as are the light fixtures you use.

• If you use incandescent bulbs over tanks, be certain that they are not close to flammable objects or plants, and that they are housed in fixtures that are appropriate in terms of wattage used and time operated.

Nutrition and Feeding Techniques

The Role of Nutrition

The role of nutrition is of extreme importance and complexity, and a discussion of it touches upon nearly every other topic addressed in this book. The overlap in certain areas will be immediately apparent. Consider, for example, the relationship between proper nutrition and good health. The influence of diet on other aspects of salamander husbandry is less evident at first glance. Captive reproduction is particularly dependent on proper nutrition and success in this area may necessitate short-term changes in the type and amount of food offered. The type of diet to be fed will also depend upon such variables as the age of the terrarium's inhabitants and the temperature at which they are maintained. The complexity of these factors increases if a variety of species of salamanders are housed together, or if they are kept with animals such as frogs, fish, or invertebrates. The type of terrarium in which the salamanders live will affect the way in which food is presented. Factors such as whether an uneaten food animal will live or die in the tank and how one will keep track of the food eaten by secretive terrarium inhabitants must all be considered.

In the material that follows, I will begin with a discussion of individual food items and will include feeding techniques and special consideration where appropriate. Unique nutritional situations, such as preparing adults for breeding, raising young, and managing the mixed-species terrarium are included under separate headings elsewhere in this book.

Types of Food

House Crickets (*Acheta domestica*)

The commercially available house cricket has been used in professional and private collections throughout the world for many years. Bearing in mind the information under the heading Vitamin and Mineral Supplementation, page 58, the house cricket can be an important food source for many salamanders. I prefer, however, to use softer-bodied prey as a staple, such as blackworms or earthworms. In the case of small or young terrestrial salamanders, such as the red-backed salamander, *Plethodon cinereus*, pinhead, and ten-day-old crickets may be one of the few practical foods to use. I have had good results raising young marbled salamanders, *Ambystoma opacum*, on a diet consisting of approximately 75 percent crickets, and many species of dendrobatid frogs are routinely kept and bred on a diet consisting exclusively of these insects.

Tip: Some things to bear in mind when using crickets are that they will drown if they cannot easily exit a water bowl (cork, bark, or plastic plants in bowls will prevent this), and smaller ones may escape through the terrarium's screen top before they are consumed. Also, uneaten crickets will quickly lose their vitamin/mineral coating (see Vitamin and Mineral Supplementation, page 58). Please also note that crickets have distinctly carnivorous leanings and may kill lethargic or injured salamanders.

How many to feed: For most salamanders, I prefer to feed several small crickets as opposed to one large one. Smaller items present more surface area to the action of digestive enzymes (one of the reasons we humans chew our food), and it seems to me that adult crickets contain a proportionately larger amount of undigestible parts (legs, wings) than do immature crickets.

Where to obtain crickets: Crickets can be purchased at pet stores, although they may be quite expensive. Most commercial cricket farms will ship quantities of several hundred, which can be stored and used as needed.

Flour Beetle Larvae

The grubs, or immature stages, of a variety of tiny beetles are readily accepted by many small salamanders. They are an important source of variety for growing animals and for those species, such as the red-backed salamander, *Plethodon cinereus*, which do not grow very large. Without them, we would be forced to rely mainly upon small crickets to feed our smaller terrestrial salamanders. I'm indebted to Bob Holland, a truly exceptional amphibian expert, for making me aware of this important food source and advising me on its culture and use. The easiest way to obtain a starter colony of small beetles (I'm uncertain as to the exact species that is most commonly encountered) is to break open some old dog biscuits (large "treat-type" bones seem to be the best). You will be amazed (and possibly distressed, if you are a dog owner) at how often you will find beetles and their larvae inside. Because they are slow moving, it is quite unlikely that any of the insects will escape. The biscuits provide all the food, moisture, and shelter that the colony needs. To concentrate the grubs so as to make finding and using them easier, break several biscuits and tap out the enclosed animals into a small plastic container. Keep only one and two biscuits in this container, so that all the grubs will concentrate in and on them. Be sure to break open the biscuits, so that the grubs will have easy access to the interior. When needed, simply tap a food-laden biscuit over a petri dish (the grubs cannot climb out of this) and place the dish in the terrarium. You can also place the grubs directly in the terrarium, but it then becomes difficult to determine if they are being eaten, as they burrow rapidly. Some species will also feed on adult beetles, so experiment with these as well.

Springtails (Collembolla sp.)

Springtails, which are tiny primitive insects, can be collected under logs and leaf litter. A strain kept by herptoculturists in Holland is larger than the native American species and breeds well in captivity. These are available commercially in Europe, and correspondence with interested parties through herpetological societies or magazines is the best method for locating a source. Due to their size, springtails are suitable for only the smallest terrestrial salamanders but are important in that food options for such animals are limited.

Mealworms (Tenebrio molitor, Zoophobias sp.)

Mealworms are the larvae of various species of beetles. I do not use them as a food source for salamanders. If you do, it would be wise to crush the head (to destroy potentially harmful mouthparts) and to use newly molted individuals. Mealworms, especially the larger *Zoophobias*, can injure or kill salamanders in poor condition.

Earthworms (Lumbricus terrestris)

The earthworm can be used as the major portion of the diet of a wide variety of salamanders, both aquatic and terrestrial. In fact, I am aware of instances in which groups of salamanders (Spotted salamander, *Ambystoma maculatum*, and Northern red salamander, *Pseudotrition ruber*) were fed nothing but earthworms from the time of metamorphosis through adulthood. All of the animals exhibited normal growth and, at age three years remain healthy and vigorous adults. According to one study, nutritional analyses of earthworms indicated that they may provide adequate levels of vitamins A and E for most captive "insectivores."

Note: You should be aware that earthworms consume dirt in their foraging activities, and thus wild-caught ones might well contain any insecticides or pollutants that are in their habitat. (The New York State Department of Environmental Conservation is examining whether a diet of earthworms contaminated with organochlorine pesticides has contributed to the decline of the striped skunk on Long Island, New York.)

Size of pieces of food: While it is best to feed an appropriately sized, entire earthworm, cut pieces can be used. Be aware that these pieces will decompose if uneaten, and uncut earthworms can drown if left underwater longer than eight hours. If your terrarium substrate is damp sphagnum moss, uneaten earthworms will generally live until captured by a salamander. If soil is used, however, they may burrow into areas where they are inaccessible to the terrariums' inhabitants.

One final word of caution: I have read that some commercial operations use the fecal waste from chicken farms to feed their earthworms. I'm not sure if this presents a potential salmonella-transmission problem so a call to your supplier might be in order.

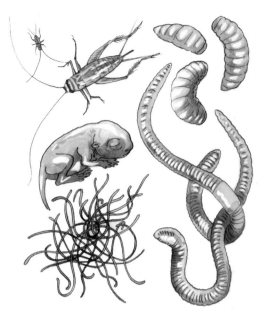

Live food for terrestrial salamanders (clockwise from the top): crickets, waxworms, earthworms, blackworms, and a newborn mouse.

Where to obtain earthworms: Earthworms can be purchased at bait stores or through commercial breeders, many of which advertise in the more popular hobbyist's magazines. They can also be collected and bred at home. A cool basement is best suited for this endeavor. They can be kept in a plastic garbage can with alternating layers of dead leaves and topsoil that is kept moist but not wet.

What earthworms eat: In addition to the leaves, earthworms will consume bread crumbs and fish food flakes, among other things. Damp burlap laid on the surface will cause earthworms to congregate below, allowing for easy collection. Having a breeding colony assures a constant supply of tiny worms, which provide a more nutritious diet for small animals than do pieces of large worms.

Sweeping a net through tall grasses can yield a variety of insects that will be eaten eagerly by salamanders.

Waxworms *(Galleria mellonella)*

Waxworms are actually caterpillars that live in beehives. They are shipped packed in sawdust and any that adheres to their bodies must be removed before they are used. They are higher in fat than most other live foods (58 percent), but little is known of the effect of fat on amphibian diets. I use them as approximately 20 percent of the diet of most terrestrial salamanders. Be sure to select an appropriately sized waxworm, as the chitenous exoskeleton appears quite thick and might present a digestive hazard. An increasing number of pet stores are selling waxworms, as are bait dealers. They require refrigeration for storage.

Whiteworms *(Enchytraeus albidus)*

Whiteworms can provide useful variety, especially for small salamanders that are often given a limited diet in captivity (see Useful Literature and Addresses, page 124, for books dealing with their husbandry). European amphibian keepers seem to use their food source to a greater extent than do those in North America. A check of international herpetological societies would most likely reveal a source.

Fruit Flies *(Drosophila melanogaster)*

Fruit flies are suitable for the tiniest salamanders and can be raised in large numbers. Flightless and large strains are available from biological supply houses.

Houseflies

Housefly and other fly larvae, or maggots, and adults can be purchased commercially through bait dealers (usually sold as "moussies" or "rat-tailed maggots") and a flightless strain is available through biological supply houses. Maggots can be offered in a low dish, but remember that they transform rapidly into adults, even at fairly cool temperatures. Adults can usually stay out of reach of most salamanders, although they cannot fly immediately after emerging from the pupae. Pupae left in a dish might therefore be an option, as would be the flightless strains.

Tip: While trapping wild flies is easy (often too easy), I would not recommend this due to the potential for diseases transmittable to people. Be careful when using these quick-moving insects—even the great Raymond Ditmars managed to accidentally fill his house with hoardes of these pests (see his autobiography), a feat I later successfully repeated with mosquitoes.

Wild-Caught Invertebrates

Wild-caught invertebrates can impart much-needed variety to captive diets, provided you are aware of the possibility of secondary insecticide poisoning (see Earthworms, page 53), and that you weed out those animals that might injure salamanders. (I once lost two frogs, both long-term captives, immediately after feeding them some Japanese beetles, *Popilla japonica*. I'm not sure if pesticides or the beetles' tough mouthparts and leg spurs were to blame.) Swinging through tall grass with a net will yield a variety of insects and spiders, but the useful and harmful ones will be mixed together. When feeding small salamanders, you can empty all of the net's contents into a container with holes that will allow only the smallest insects to exit. Commercial or homemade light traps can also be used and are less likely to snare insects that can harm salamanders.

Slugs are eagerly taken by many salamanders, as are smaller snails; however, it may be possible that certain snails can transmit parasites to salamanders. Aphids can be an important source of variety for small, terrestrial species, but I've noticed a tremendous decline in aphid numbers in New York over the past two decades.

Boards placed on the ground will attract a variety of invertebrates, which can be harvested as needed. Grasshoppers can be collected or purchased and bred year-round.

Live food for aquatic salamanders (clockwise from the top): brine shrimp, daphnia, mosquito larvae, and a guppy.

Brine Shrimp, Daphnia, Aquatic Isopods, Mosquito Larva

These tiny aquatic creatures have a place in the diet of newly hatched aquatic salamander larvae.

Brine shrimp are one of the few small-sized live food sources that are commercially available. As soon as the larvae's size permits, however, I switch them to chopped blackworms, a more substantial meal that allows for greater growth. Brine shrimp must be rinsed to remove salt traces, and wild-caught invertebrates should be checked so that larval predators such as predaceous diving beetles can be removed. Adult brine shrimp can be purchased from most pet stores. Eggs are sold bottled (they remain viable for years when dried out), as are a variety of hatchery kits. The kits use light, which attracts shrimp, to separate shrimp from eggs and concentrate them for easy collection.

Daphnia is cultured by placing some hay in a container of pond water, which is kept in a sunny location. In the alternative, a small amount of pond water can be introduced into the tank as needed. Due to its small size, daphnia is suitable for only the tiniest of aquatic larvae.

Mosquito larva can be collected with a finely meshed dip net from stagnant pools of water. If you are not fortunate enough to have your own stagnant pool of water nearby, put out some cans of water and sit back and wait, or check wherever water collects in temporary settings such as inside old tires, refrigerator bins, etc. Be aware that mosquito larvae transform into adults rapidly, and check with your local health department to determine if mosquito-borne diseases are a problem in your area. Be sure that you can recognize mosquito larvae. As a youngster, I couldn't, and once filled the house with hoards of hungry mosquitoes—much to the horror of my sister, who is allergic to their bites!

Blackworms

I have successfully used blackworms as the sole diet for Mexican axolotl, *Ambystoma mexicanum*, larvae and include them as a regular part of the diets of most of the species that I work with. I much prefer them to the more familiar tubifex worms, which are harvested from sewage-laden waters and which have been tentatively implicated in amphibian gastrointestinal disorders. Blackworms are increasingly available in pet stores and will live for at least two weeks in the refrigerator if their water is changed daily. (Dead worms float when the water is disturbed and can be poured off.) Uneaten blackworms will live in an aquarium until captured. They will also thrive in damp sphagnum moss and can therefore be fed to terrestrial salamanders as well. Blackworms clump together in bare-bottom tanks, even if cut into small pieces. On several occasions, I have found salamander larvae dead with clumps of cut blackworms lodged in their throats. The use of a commercial floating worm feeder will limit this, especially if it is positioned by a filter's outflow. The worms do not clump together on a gravel substrate.

Crayfish

The hellbender, *Cryptobranchus alleganiensis*, sirens, *siren* sp., amphiumas, *Amphiuma* sp., and mudpuppies, *Necturus* sp., are reputed to feed heavily upon crayfish in the wild. A three-toed amphiuma under my care, which would attack anything (including the hand that fed it!), refused hard-shelled crayfish but would consume soft, newly shed ones. Analysis has shown crayfish to contain particularly high concentrations of vitamin E and they should be offered to the aforementioned species. Unless the crayfish are soft (recently molted), the claws should be removed. I have been informed that American bullfrogs, *Rana catesbeiana*, do well on a diet containing a large proportion of crayfish. Most commercial bait dealers sell crayfish, and they store well in the refrigerator.

Fish

Whole fish are an excellent food for those salamanders that will consume vertebrates. Fish, much like all vertebrate prey, supply a calcium:phosphorus ratio of approximately 2:1, which is the level that should be given to captive amphibians. Theoretically, whole freshwater fish would appear to be nutritionally complete for certain aquatic salamanders. However, it is unlikely that any species subsists solely on fish in the wild, and I'm unable to say what the long-term effects of such a diet might be. There is currently speculation in the zoological parks community that insectivorous lizards (salamanders are less studied) develop corneal opacities and other problems when fed too many vertebrates. I have found that most aquatic and semiaquatic salamanders will accept suitably sized guppies, minnows, shiners, goldfish, and, for the largest species, trout.

Where to obtain food fish: Most useful food fish can be purchased at pet stores or through bait dealers. If you use large amounts, it will be less expensive if you order large quantities through a wholesale dealer and store them. Goldfish, minnows, and shiners generally require a cool, well-aerated storage facilities, such as a Living Stream tank (see page 28).

Wild fish can be netted with a seine net, or a minnow trap can be left in a suitable location. Be aware that most states strictly regulate the taking of all fish, including those listed as "bait." Regarding goldfish, it should be noted that mata-mata turtles, *Chelus fimbriatus*, consistently die after several years on a goldfish-only diet. When fed pond-raised fathead minnows, *Pimephales promelas*, and golden shiners, *Notemigonus crysoleucas*, the turtles do very well in captivity.

Amphibians

Amphibian eggs and larvae are most likely important prey items for wild salamanders. I do not, however, advocate collecting them as food, due to the precarious state of populations of even once-common species. However, a well-fed breeding pair of Mexican axolotls, *Ambystoma mexicanum*, will produce large numbers of eggs and larvae for about five months of the year. Also, larval salamanders will consume each other unless given plenty of food and shelter. Where it is impossible to raise the large number of young produced, this predilection might prove useful for both salamander and salamander-keeper. The use of adult salamanders as food is largely precluded, as we do not know the effects of their toxic skin secretions on other animals. This fact was brought home to me when, as a boy, I fed an injured red-spotted newt, *Notophalmus viridescens*, (aquatic phase) to a marine toad, Bufo *marinus*. The toad, a large, robust beast capable of downing a small rat, ate the tiny newt and immediately rolled over and died.

Rodents

Pink mice are eagerly accepted by the Mexican axolotl, *Ambystoma mexicanum*, the Pacific giant salamander, *Dicamptodon ensatus*, and the tiger salamander, *Ambystoma tigrinum*. Larger species such as the three-toed amphiuma, *Amphiuma tridactylum*, will even consume adult mice, although I prefer the hairless pinkies for these also. Please read the cautions under the heading Fish before considering rodents as a food source. There is increasing evidence that links high fat foods with corneal opacities in insectivorous lizards. Mice are available from most pet stores. I do not recommend trapping your own, due to the wide variety of diseases and parasites you may contract.

Trout Chow and Other Commercially Prepared Foods

Trout chow appears to have great potential as a staple diet for those salamanders that will accept nonliving prey (generally those species that rely on their sense of smell to find aquatic prey). One benefit of a diet based on trout chow is that it might provide most of the nutrients necessary for health and reproduction and eliminate the need for hit-or-miss experimentation with a variety of live foods. Even if we know an animal's nutritional needs, the basic nutritional make-up of food animals will vary with their diet, age, and reproductive condition. My experience, along with the anecdotal information that I have heard from others, indicates that trout chow can be used as a nearly complete diet for at least one salamander and perhaps several species of turtle. (Please bear in mind, however, that this information has not been quantified by experimentation, nor do I know how far one can stretch the comparison between the dietary needs of trout and salamanders.) I have raised many newly hatched

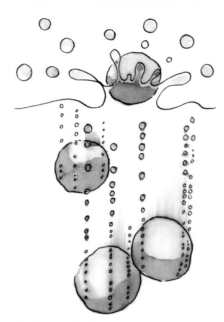

Early reports indicate that trout chow may be a simple and effective way to feed certain salamanders.

Vitamin and Mineral Supplementation

Dietary supplementation for captive salamanders is a poorly studied topic. Perhaps the greatest stumbling block in deciding what, if any, supplements to use is the fact that we do not know what constitutes a balanced diet for most species of salamander. The little we do know is mainly drawn from years of trial and error. In the previous section I have drawn attention to some examples of apparently complete diets.

There are several approaches to providing a diet containing all of the nutrients needed for health, growth, and reproduction. It is important to note that each of these functions may require changes in the diet. For example, an adult salamander may survive for years on a diet that would not support reproduction or larval growth.

Variety

The other approach to feeding captive amphibians is to provide as wide a variety of food as is possible, with or without supplements, with the hope that most of what the animal needs will be found in the sum total of the food offered. Studies of free-living amphibians indicate that many consume a wide variety of prey. Over the course of a year, the diet will usually vary with the abundance of prey. One item might dominate for a period of time, while daily variety might be the order of the day during another season. Thus, while we cannot hope to mimic nature, whatever variety is offered should add to the captive's well-being.

Food Animals' Diet

Food animals should, where possible, be fed a nutritious diet for a time before being offered to your salamanders. This will increase their nutritional value. Studies have shown that two

Mexican axolotls, *Ambystoma mexicanum*, on a diet of 50 percent trout chow. When the animals were about 1 inch (2.5 cm) long, I switched to 90 percent trout chow. The adults breed each year on this diet, slowing down only if I cut back on the total amount of trout chow offered. The animals are as large and robust as any I've seen and I've observed no problems in the five years during which I've maintained the colony in this fashion. This group will swim to the surface of a deep tank to eat floating trout chow. A sinking variety of trout chow is also available, although it seems to break down quickly in water.

Other pelleted foods that hold promise are Tetramin's Reptomin and Purina's Turtle Chow.

days is the optimal time for crickets to be allowed to feed, in terms of imparting to them greater nutritional value. Tetramin tropical fish flakes are readily consumed by crickets and earthworms, as is trout chow. This is a good way of providing some of the benefits of such prepared diets to salamanders that will consume only living prey. Crickets should also have a source of moisture, such as oranges, green vegetables, or sweet potatoes, which also provide a nutritional benefit. Ground limestone should be mixed into the food given to such animals as crickets and earthworms. I use a ratio of 1:1 trout chow:limestone (by weight) when feeding crickets.

Limestone (available through garden supply stores as limecrest) can be placed into a bag with food animals and shaken over them. I do not add it to the diets of salamanders that regularly consume fish, as most vertebrate prey provides a calcium:phosphorus ratio of 2:1, which seems to be an adequate dietary calcium level.

Warning: Crickets and other food animals will lose their vitamin/mineral coating if they wander about in the terrarium for any length of time without being eaten. It is therefore, best to provide food at a time when you know the salamanders will feed immediately or to feed them by forceps or hand, if possible, or to confine food to a dish with the powdered supplements. Also, feeding too many food items at once will result in uneaten ones losing their supplement coating. I use a commercial vitamin/mineral supplement, such as Red-Cal or Nekton-Rep once a week for most animals (on alternate weeks only for those animals consuming vertebrates or an extremely varied diet). You might experiment a bit with the aforementioned recommendations, depending upon the diet offered. For example, a three-toed amphiuma, *Amphiuma means*, consuming a diet consisting of minnows, crayfish, earthworms, blackworms, waxworms, crickets, snails, and pink mice would likely need no supplementation. Nor would a Mexican axolotl, *Ambystoma mexicanum*, living on a diet of trout chow and an occasional fish or earthworm. However, red-backed salamanders, *Plethonodon cinereus*, provided with only ten-day-old crickets might need to have supplementation with most of their meals.

Be sure to think about raising other nontraditional food sources, especially those that can provide variety to animals that are usually kept on a limited diet in captivity, and to share your discoveries with others, including myself.

Health

An Important Note About Amphibian Health Care*

Please be aware of the following:

• A relationship with a veterinarian well versed in amphibian medicine is an absolute necessity for the successful long-term propagation of salamanders, but, unfortunately, such persons are few and far between.

• One should bear in mind when considering amphibian medications that the skin of these animals is extremely porous, which will affect the types and amount of medication that can be used. Many commercially available medications designed for tropical aquarium fish play an important role in amphibian medicine. Although I have had excellent results using the dosages recommended for fish, the safest method is to start with a slightly diluted concentration. The main reason for this is that aquatic salamanders in particular will have a greater surface area for absorption of the medication if it is administered in water. The entire skin surface will allow transfer of the medication.

• Basic hygiene is the starting point for avoiding illnesses and, in some cases, for treatment.

• As mentioned earlier, bottled water (such as Deer Park) should always be on hand for an emergency, as when you need to flush ammonia or heavy metals from an animal's system.

---

*Large portions of the following section, especially as concerns the specifics of using medications, were adapted from "Amphibians," by Dr. Bonnie L. Raphael (*Exotic Pet Medicine*, 23(6): 1271, 1993. I am grateful for her permission to use this information, and for her counsel in this area.

• Proper temperature and humidity levels and the absence of stress will go a long way in preventing diseases.

• One must also be careful in actually administering medication, especially injectables. The mucus-coated skin is the main defense against a variety of harmful microorganisms. In fact, many times an injury or a cut will lead to death because of the invasion of opportunistic bacteria.

• Handling of the animal should be done as carefully and as little as possible and with wet hands only or, if possible, with a plastic water-filled bag.

• Salamanders should never be caught in a stiff nylon net that would rub off the mucus covering and leave it open to secondary infections.

• When injecting the salamander one should note on the animal treatment card—which should always be present—into what leg the injection was administered. The next time, the leg should be rotated to avoid damaging one particular site with many injections. Injections are always given in the front leg of salamanders.

Bacteria

Aeromonas hydrophila

This is a common gram negative bacteria that is one of the main culprits behind a condition known as *septicemia*. It is contagious and can be transmitted by contact with infected water. One of the symptoms is a skin hemorrhage, a reddish area that becomes progressively worse and where the skin eventually sloughs off. In its terminal state, the animal may twitch, convulse, and become comatose. Generally, we apply the term *red leg* to the condition when it occurs in amphibians. Species other than *Aeromonas* bacteria may also be implicated. Generally, the animal also decreases its activities, loses weight, and becomes dull in coloration. Improved sanitation is the first immediate step to take. Hands must be washed between handling each animal. Environmental conditions such as poor hygiene will contribute to *Aeromonas* outbreaks. In some amphibian species, *Aeromonas* infection or red leg is cured or prevented by refrigeration at 39 to 41°F (4–5°C) for two weeks. This has been successful treatment for the Mexican axolotl, *Ambystoma mexicanum*, and also for the leopard frog, *Rana pipiens*. While lacerated skin would lead one to believe that *Aeromonas* is the culprit, a definite diagnosis can be made by blood culture. There is evidence that, at least in frogs, animals may be carriers of *Aeromonas* bacteria but not exhibit symptoms.

Salmonella spp.

Salmonella was discussed earlier in relation to possible hazards to people. It must be kept in mind that *Salmonella* is not the only pathogen that can be transmitted from animals to people and that strict hygiene in both dealing with your animal and concerning yourself are absolutely essential. An animal affected with *Salmonella* will generally go off feed. The animal will become very lethargic and thin, and possibly will develop diarrhea. Diarrhea, however, is difficult to observe in salamanders, especially aquatic species where the waste products are generally in a liquid form. Blood tests will reveal that an infected animal is generally anemic. A variety of antibiotics has been successfully used against *Salmonella*. Gentamicin has proven effective and should be followed by baths in methylene blue and/or acriflavine.

Mycobacteria spp.

Infection by *Mycobacteria* will manifest itself as small skin nodules and the animal will develop pneumonia. The animal's appearance will change, and it will stop feeding and probably exhibit abnormal behavior patterns, such as resting where it normally does not, lying out in the open, not venturing out to feed at night, etc. Medications that have proven successful in some cases are Isolate Amikacin and Enrofloxacin.

Chlamydia spp.

Chlamydia infection will cause edema, so the afflicted animal will appear swollen all over, unlike the localized abdominal swelling condition that can be caused by gas. Skin sloughing and hemorrhages, not unlike those seen in red leg, will appear. Animals thus afflicted will also become lethargic and cease feeding. Oxytetracycline has proven an effective treatment if administered early.

Gas Bubble Disease

Gas bubble disease results when amphibians are kept in water that has become supersaturated with any of the gases normally found in the air, that is oxygen, carbon dioxide, nitrogen, or argon. In natural situations, supersaturation often occurs during the summer because the increased temperature of the water results in a decreased solubility of gases. Bacterial action and plant growth may also contribute to this condition in both natural and artificial systems.

Perhaps the most common way for a supersaturated condition to occur in captivity is air being introduced into the system through leaks around the pump or holes in tubing, loose valves, and even aeration purposely put into the tank for the animals. In general, except for animals from very fast-moving waters, most salamanders should be kept in water that is only moderately aerated. In a supersaturated situation, bubbles may form in the blood of the salamander. Such bubbles are called emboli. Gas bubbles may also be formed in the animal's tissues. Often these can be seen, with the naked eye, just below the skin. Bubbles may be seen in the eye or may congregate in the abdomen where swelling will occur, and also in the webbing between the toes of aquatic amphibians. Death results from the internal accumulation of gas or, commonly, from a secondary bacterial infection. The agent of infection is usually *Aeromonas hydrophila*.

Symptoms: Animals affected with gas bubble disease may float and be unable to submerge and will often have trouble feeding and moving about normally. Equilibrium will also be affected. The animal will have difficulty swimming and will occasionally rise up tail first to the surface, and then be unable to submerge for a short time. Eventually, affected animals may just float about on the surface until they die. The internal bubbles cause rupturing of capillaries and hemorrhages occur under the skin. These eventually enlarge and form patches of necrotic skin. Typical symptoms of red leg, or septicemia are generally visible at this point, and indeed the *Aeromonas* bacteria is usually a culprit.

Removing the gas: While supersaturated water can lose gas to the atmosphere, this will work well only in a small system where there is time to let the water sit. However, a large tank with a constant inflow of water, such as one might set up to keep Japanese or Chinese giant salamanders, will need a different approach. One of the most effective ways to remove the gases from supersaturated water is to allow the water to enter the system by trickling through 4-foot-high (1.2 m) PVC pipe filled with small stones. Allowing water to enter as a fine mist, as, for example, using a nozzle set on a spray setting, will also allow much of the gases to dissipate before they enter the system.

If you are involved with large aquatic systems, you would be well advised to consult a fish hatchery. Commercial fish hatcheries have long recognized gas bubble disease as a problem in fish culture, and would be able to provide you with alternative means of avoiding the problem. In addition to removing the source of the gas saturation, antibiotics will need to be given to animals to kill the bacteria involved.

Fungal Infections

Unsanitary environmental conditions predispose an animal to fungal infections. Also, a depressed immune system will allow microorganisms to attack an animal that might otherwise fight off the infection on its own. Diagnoses of fungal infections are accomplished by biopsy, although in some cases symptoms are fairly typical and biopsies may not be necessary.

Saprolegniasis

Saprolegniasis is one of the more common mycotic infections of aquatic amphibians. The usual culprit is the fungus *Saprolegnia*, although as many as 20 species of aquatic fungi may actually cause the condition. Saprolegniasis, a disease that is relatively common among tropical fish, has only recently been diagnosed in amphibians. Typically, first symptoms are a cotton-like growth on the animal's skin or occasionally only on the gills. The skin below the growth may be inflamed or ulcerated. Animals afflicted with this condition will become weak and thin, will regurgitate, and seem to have trouble breathing. *Saprolegnia* is present in most aquatic systems and may begin to cause problems when the mucus on the salamander's skin is removed. As discussed earlier, this can be caused by handling the animal with dry hands or a nylon net. In contrast to what we have seen for *Aeromonas* infections, *Saprolegnia* seems to survive poorly at higher temperatures, or at least at temperatures over 70°F (21°C). Bacteria such as *Aeromonas* are also generally in the environment and may use the ulcerated skin as an attack site. The most effective treatment for Saprolegniasis is benzalkonium chloride, keeping the animal in water and medicated until symptoms disappear. Water should be changed frequently, no less than three times per week.

Parasites

Free-living amphibians normally are host to a variety of parasites. Whether or not this condition will become dangerous or pathogenic depends on a variety of circumstances, such as individual resistance of the host, the concentration of parasites, and very importantly, for the captive situation, the captive environment, and nutrition. Many parasites are extremely resistant to treatment and reinfection is often the rule. In these cases, periodic dewormings may be necessary to control the condition. In other words, it is expected that the animal will have parasites in its system and will need to be treated at regular intervals.

Protozoa exist in a variety of aquatic and semiaquatic environments and are the causative agents of a tremendous number of diseases in amphibians. Some, such as *Trypanosoma diemictyli* are always fatal and not treatable at the present time. *Charchesium* and *Vorticella* cause a fuzzy covering on the gills and will kill the animal by preventing proper respiration. A bath in distilled water for two to three hours and in a 0.6 percent sodium chloride solution for three to five days has proven effective, as has copper sulfate treatments.

Velvet Disease

Velvet disease is caused by a flagellated protozoa known as *Oodinium pillularis*. Generally, the disease begins as a small fuzzy gray area on the skin or occasionally on the gills. If the disease concentrates on the gills, the animal will be seen gulping for air as its ability to respirate will be severely curtailed. A distilled water bath for two to three hours followed by a sodium chloride bath for three to five days (0.6 percent solution) or treatment with copper sulfate is recommended.

Calcium/Phosphorus Ratio

It has been shown for many reptiles that if the ratio of calcium to phosphorus is less than 1.2:1, deformed or soft bones will result due to a calcium deficiency. The animal will also be subject to fractures even when going about its normal activities and will tend to be less active and weak. In the advanced stages it will exhibit tetany. This condition is manifested by an animal being unable to right itself in the proper position and also by twitching of the toes and limbs. At this stage calcium injections (calcium gluconate) are the only means of effecting a cure. In the early stages supplementation with calcium carbonate will help to prevent or reverse the process.

Vitamin Imbalances

Vitamin D

Many reptiles raised without an ultraviolet light source or without vitamin D in the diet will exhibit symptoms similar to those described for a calcium deficiency. Many species of reptiles are not able to produce vitamin D in the absence of a proper UV source. This varies a great deal from species to species. Some animals can use dietary vitamin D. Access to sunlight or proper artificial UV radiation and supplementing a diet with vitamin D has worked for a variety of reptile species. Most salamanders do not bask and, in fact, chemicals providing protection against ultraviolet light have been found in the eggs of salamanders that lay in an open situation, indicating that at least certain wavelengths of UV radiation may be harmful to these animals. A similar UV protective has been found in the skin of some frogs, but not in salamanders. I am unable to find any evidence that salamanders would require UV in order to avoid a vitamin D deficiency. Indeed, soft bones, fractures, etc. rarely show up in salamanders. Perhaps studies should be done concerning those species that lay in shallow open situations under water or on the larvae of such species.

Vitamin A

An excess of vitamin A in the diet will cause liver damage and eventually death. In salamander husbandry this has generally been a problem only in laboratory colonies of axolotls, *Ambystoma mexicanum*, where it has been standard practice to feed raw liver as the sole diet. Raw liver is not really needed in the diet of salamanders and it is probably easier to feed large axolotl colonies trout chow that, as has been discussed, seems to be a complete diet. It might be possible that overuse of commercial reptile supplements will be linked to a vitamin A excess and liver damage, although I am not aware that such cases have been reported.

Vitamin B

A diet high in fish has been implicated in vitamin B deficiencies. I believe that this is only a problem with saltwater fish, which should not form the bulk of any salamander's diet. Vitamin B deficiencies show up as general weakness, ataxia, and paralysis. Injectable vitamin B_1 supplements in the amount of 25 mg of vitamin B_1 per kilogram of fish can be used to reverse a vitamin B deficiency.

Chemicals and Other Substances

Chlorine, ammonia, pesticides, disinfectants, or nearly any other substance that is in the water can injure or kill salamanders. A variety of heavy metals, some of which are found in water pipes, may also be fatal. If the system has copper, zinc, or lead (generally found in very old buildings), water should be allowed to run for up to one-half hour before being used. Test results have shown that copper levels vary significantly between water that has been lying in the pipes overnight and water that has run for several minutes before being used. Copper is a medicine or a parasite toxicant at some levels but at higher levels it kills fish and amphibians. As has been discussed earlier, spring water baths can be used to detoxify animals that have been exposed to ammonia or other chemical poisoning. Ammonia levels are raised by feces and uneaten food in the environment. It has been suggested that a bath of 10 percent thiosulfate can also be used to treat the effects of chlorine or ammonia poisoning.

Beware of using plastic containers to carry amphibians. If such containers have held soaps or other disinfectants, it will be very difficult to make them safe to use. Such chemicals tend to remain in plastic for a long time and are very difficult to rinse out and remove. I am aware of several cases of frogs and salamanders having been poisoned after being placed in apparently clean containers that had previously contained soap or other commercial disinfectants.

While on the topic, I should point out that rock and wood, especially cork bark, are also likely to absorb and retain harmful chemicals or bacteria. Cleaning and disinfecting materials such as wood, rock, and plastic is best done by using very hot water and salt. If something stronger is needed, laundry bleach is a powerful disinfectant; it also, rinses off easily and more completely than other cleaners.

Your Role—Research

It should be noted that, because of the paucity of research in this area, there is a great deal that can be done by the serious hobbyist. One area that should be examined closely, and that is fairly accessible to everyone, is the use of the variety of tropical fish medications for treatment of diseases in amphibians. Certain aspects of the internal workings of fish and amphibians are similar, and I myself have had a good deal of success with medications such as acriflavine and methylene blue in the treatment of various fungal problems in amphibians. To be safe, one might start with a lower dosage than that recommended for the treatment of fish. Amphibians, especially aquatic ones, take in a good deal of water through the skin and cloaca and thus have a larger surface area for absorption of the medication than do most fish.

Another very interesting approach is the use of temperature in controlling or even curing disease in amphibians. Commercial laboratories have had success in controlling septicemia infections in leopard frogs, *Rana pipiens*, by keeping the animals at 40°F (4°C) for several days. These temperatures can be reached in the normal home refrigerator. I am aware of several cases of Mexican axolotls, *Ambystoma mexicanum*, that would become bloated and float to the surface when held at temperatures of 75°F (24°C) or higher. The condition was undiagnosed. When kept at temperatures below 60°F (15°C), the animals moved about normally and did fine for years. I am also familiar with several cases of cold adapted aquatic amphibians that were submitted for necropsies when they were found apparently dead. In three cases, a night in the necropsy refrigerator seemed to cure the animal. The species involved were the hellbender, *Cryptobranchus alleganiensis*, and the Mexican axolotl, *Ambstoma mexicanum*.

Obtaining Salamanders

As stated earlier, I feel that people in the private sector should refrain completely from collecting salamanders. There is enough of a variety of captive-bred species available to provide for many lifetimes of intense study. Collection, where absolutely necessary, should be only in connection with an organized conservation-oriented project administered by a zoological park, museum, or government body.

Zoological parks will sometimes form cooperative breeding agreements with serious, competent nonprofessionals. Increasingly, captive animal populations are being professionally managed by zoo-based "species survival plans." Mating and inter-zoo transfers are organized so as to preserve the greatest possible percentage of the population's genetic diversity. Husbandry protocol and *in situ* conservation programs are also administered. While there is currently little emphasis on amphibians in general and salamanders in particular, this situation will change. Herein lie great opportunities for advanced hobbyists to indulge their passions while making real contributions to important conservation efforts.

Federal and local governmental confiscations of animals illegally put into the food or pet trade currently account for a significant portion of the unexpected animals with which zoos must deal each year. In very limited circumstances, these animals may be sent to private individuals while trials are pending or for permanent placement. Incorporation into this process is most easily attained by involvement with serious local herpetological organizations, zoological parks, and aquariums and museums.

It is important to establish a good working relationship with the pet store or private breeder with which you deal. This will enable you to ascertain necessary background information concerning specimens in which you are interested. Reputable stores and dealers know the importance of such information and should be happy to provide it.

Choosing an Individual

The choice of an individual animal is made after deciding what species to work with. The sex of the individual is important, of course, depending upon your breeding requirements. Sex is not always determinable outside of the breeding season. (See the sections on the species in which you are interested for specifics.) Animals should be well fed but not obese. It takes a good deal of practice to determine the difference between the two, especially with the more slenderly built species.

The area above the hips is one place to look to determine whether the animal is too thin. Bones that are noticeable there usually indicate that an animal is underfed. This is especially useful for animals that are very thinly built. A thin animal might indicate only that it is not being fed enough, or it could be an indication of parasites or disease.

Bloat: One also needs to distinguish between an animal with a full stomach and one that is bloated. Bloating is generally exhibited as a swelling along the sides of the animal, as well as in the stomach area. Edema would be indicated by a generalized swelling throughout the body and aquatic species will have difficulty swimming. Those with bloating due to gas will also not be able to submerge properly. Again, experience is pretty much the only way to distinguish these conditions from a full stomach. Ideally, an animal to be taken into the collection should be observed feeding. However, this is not always possible as many do not feed on demand or in situations of bright light or where they are being observed (especially animals newly taken into captivity).

As much background information as possible should be obtained on the individual that you wish to purchase. This is vital for breeding purposes, and it is especially important in terms of the animal's range. Many species are broken into various widely distributed populations, and each population will have certain characteristics that should be preserved by breeding only with animals from the same population. Age and past dietary consideration are also important to determine. Even the most lethargic of species should exhibit some response to handling, and should become alert when disturbed and exhibit escape behavior. Tears or redness in the skin are especially important to check for. Salamanders are extremely sensitive to injuries to the skin, which often become infected quickly.

Tip: Animals kept in an overcrowded situation should definitely be avoided, as many of the problems they may have—such as parasites—might be undetectable through a casual observation. Generally, if they are kept very crowded, one can assume that there will be problems. Removal of the slime coating of animals through too much handling or rubbing in crowded conditions will result in infections.

Laws and Regulations

A variety of county, state, city, federal, and international laws regulate the legality of keeping animals in captivity. Until recently, little was done in regard to regulating the trade in amphibians; this is now changing. Merely because an animal is offered for sale, even in a reputable store, does not mean that it is legal to keep, and the fact that it was captive bred is also not always enough to guarantee legality. Also, since rules change, the safest method would be to call your state Department of Environmental Conservation and the local office of the U.S. Fish and Wildlife Service. Both of these agencies would be able to tell you what laws they have on the books concerning the species in which you are interested and should be able to point you toward ways of discovering other applicable laws and regulations.

Eastern newts (Notophtalmus viridescens). *Make sure that you can recognize healthy specimens (top). Avoid thin, weak salamanders (center), and bloated creatures that are unable to submerge (bottom).*

67

HOW-TO:
Transporting and Establishing the New Animal

A Styrofoam cooler chest, freezer packs, and (for very special applications) a hot water bottle can enable you to maintain the proper temperature while transporting specimens.

What to Use to Transport

The stress level experienced during transportation can be significant. After a move, parasites and other pathogens that are normally harmless to the animal might flare up due to the stressed condition. Transportation should, of course, be as short as possible and should occur in a darkened condition. The animal should be able to hide. Most salamanders do not feel that they are hidden without some sort of contact with a substrate. In this regard, small plastic shelters should not be used in the transportation container because they can move around and injure the animal. Rather, for terrestrial species, sphagnum moss is ideal as the salamanders can burrow into it, be out of sight, and have the feeling of contact. For aquatic species, shallow water with plastic plants floating in it will provide the same sense of security.

Plastic bags make ideal transportation containers, as do pillowcases for terrestrial species. When using pillowcases, be sure to turn the pillowcase inside out as threads within the case will entangle delicate legs and cause injury.

I generally avoid using glass or plastic tanks, as stressed animals will rub against the glass during the trip, often resulting in injury.

Controlling Temperature

The transportation container should be packed inside a styrofoam cooler so that temperature can be controlled during the trip. In the rare event that warming is necessary, a hot water bottle can be used. To cool the styrofoam container, one can use freezer icepacks. Be sure to take temperatures before the trip so that you can determine how much of the heating or cooling element to use and how long it retains its effectiveness.

Transporting salamanders. A pillow case partially filled with sphagnum moss makes an effective carrier for terrestrial species. Use a sturdy plastic bag partially filled with water for aquatic species.

Establishing the New Animal

Animals new to your collection should be quarantined before being placed with others. This will allow you to observe peculiarities of the individual's feeding and behavior and to monitor its health. The standard procedure in zoological parks is to keep an animal separate until three fecal samples have been shown negative for parasites. This would be the ideal situation in captivity. If fecal exams are not performed, a quarantine of at least one month is required. If your animal does not actively feed while you are watching, use a food source that is easy to count and for the animal to find—for example, crickets as opposed to earthworms. Disturb the animal as little as possible and experiment with a variety of foods. This is especially important since it will be easier to keep track of what's going on while the animal is alone. Once it is put into a community tank, such detailed observations will be more difficult.

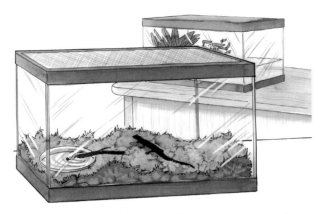

The isolation tank—essential equipment when you are introducing new animals to your terrarium.

Be aware that salamanders can become fixated on a specific food in the wild or in the captive situation. Also, certain animals exhibit cycles or phases when they will prefer one type of food or another. This might be linked to availability in the wild, or perhaps it is a method of assuring proper nutrition.

Tip: Earthworms will live well in cool sphagnum moss or soil.

This will allow shy animals to capture them during the evening, assuming that the worms cannot burrow completely out of reach. They will also survive for at least 24 hours and sometimes up to 48 hours in well-aerated cool water so that aquatic species that will not feed while you are present will also have the chance to eat.

The Ideal Situation—Studying Wild Populations

Natural populations of salamanders tend to be very stable in terms of their location. Studying them in many ways resembles the captive situation; however, there is nothing to compare to actually going out and learning about these creatures in the wild. A side benefit of spending time outside is the variety of other fascinating creatures and observations that will come your way. Research, as well as conversations with local biologists, will help to prepare you for this phase of your study. Very little is known about the life histories of even the most widespread species. Particularly lacking are studies that span the entire year, and these are necessary to fully understand any animal.

A thorough study of any salamander will also contribute to your knowledge (and, potentially, to that of others of the entire system they inhabit). The biomass of terrestrial salamanders in northeastern forests can be equal to or greater than the biomass of all other vertebrates in that system; therefore, their effect on the ecosystem is tremendous. As an adjunct to your observations, the physical parameters such as water chemistry, temperature, humidity levels, etc. throughout the year should be monitored and analyzed to help you to understand their effects on the salamanders' lifestyle. Observations in the field will also help with captive maintenance and should provide answers to many of the problems that plague us at present. This will do away with a lot of the haphazard guesswork that is now in use. I would caution against making manipulations in the field without research and discussions with field biologists actively involved in your area of study.

Note: Many professionals who work with amphibians are underfunded and welcome competent and enthusiastic help in the field. Speak to local nature centers, zoological parks, and universities to determine who is working in your area, and make yourself available to them. You will be surprised at how often there will be something that you can do, even if you lack formal training in this area. Many of the details of fieldwork can be accomplished by non-professionals and will add greatly to the store of information being collected on free-living individuals. Most professionals simply do not have the time to collect the vast array of information necessary for a complete field study.

Care of the Various Species

Ambystomatidae

Mexican Axolotl
(Ambystoma mexicanum)

Range and habitat: This member of the family Ambystomatidae (the mole salamander) is nearly extinct in the wild. Its entire natural habitat consists of Lake Xochimilco and Lake Chalco, both southeast of Mexico City. Lake Chalco has been drained and Lake Xochimilco has been reduced to a series of irrigation channels. The present status of this creature in the wild is unknown. Some are still thought to exist within the canal system or in garden ponds in the surrounding area. Although this animal has been known to science for some time, and strangely enough is an important research animal in laboratories, the first wild study appears to have been commenced in the mid-1980s. There is a good deal of confusion as to species integrity because Mexican axolotls will interbreed with the neotenic stages of the closely related tiger salamander, *Ambystoma tigrinum,* and this does in fact appear to have happened among the first batch of animals that were sent out of Mexico to Europe for study. Axolotls and closely related species were, and possibly still are, human dietary items as well. Their importance in developmental biology and in embryology research has resulted in the establishment of huge captive populations, but again the genetic makeup of these individuals is uncertain. Animals offered for sale through the trade are almost certainly captive bred.

Description: Normally colored olive brown with branching reddish gills, captive bred color strains are available, including leucistic, albino, black, yellow, and piebald. The axolotl is completely aquatic and is termed an "inducible obligate neotene." The natural situation is for it to be neotenic, that is, retaining larval characteristics such as external gills and living an aquatic lifestyle, but the administration of thyroid hormones will cause it to undergo metamorphosis and become a land-dwelling animal. However, animals stimulated to become land dwelling generally die shortly thereafter. This is in contrast to certain of its close relatives such as tiger salamanders, *Ambystoma tigrinum,* which are termed "faculative neotenes," in that transformation to the adult form can occur under favorable conditions, but in some circumstances the animals will reproduce in the larval form. Such neotenic tiger salamanders are the animals that are believed to have bred with the Mexican axolotls and to have produced the hybrids which are in evidence today.

Care: The axolotl makes a fairly hardy aquarium animal and is a good one to start with in order to sharpen one's breeding skills. It does best in cool water. Despite the fact it is from Mexico, its natural habitat is at a high elevation where the water is always cool. Although I know of people keeping axolotls at higher temperatures,

A normal axolotl is olive brown.

they do much better at about 70°F (19°C) with a drop to 52°F (10°C) during the winter. This drop in temperature, especially if it occurs during the normal winter period, will stimulate reproduction. A cool basement is ideal for keeping them year-round and if there is a window available, the natural light cycle will be enough to stimulate normal reproduction. Animals under my care are fairly seasonal in their breeding, laying eggs from January through March occasionally into April. Water temperature at this time is generally 56°F (12°C). While they can be slowly acclimated to a variety of water types, they do best in soft water with a pH of 6.9 to 7.6. I have seen evidence that hard water can damage the gills, as can high acidity. They have large appetites, especially when growing, and water changes should be frequent. I have observed several animals to float, especially at high temperatures, 76°F (22°C) or above. *Saproneglia* infection is a possible cause. The animals sink and swim and feed normally when the temperature is dropped below 70°F (19°C). An overzealous acquaintance of mine keeps one such afflicted animal in the vegetable bin of his refrigerator. The animal has apparently been living and thriving there for many years, much to the dismay of the other members of the household.

Axolotls are one of the few species of salamander that seems to do fine without any shelter. Well-acclimatized individuals do not appear at all stressed by being kept in a bare tank. They will respond to your presence upon opening the lid by swimming to the top if they are accustomed to eating floating food. In a crowded tank, however, the presence of shelters will help to alleviate aggression between the animals.

Breeding: Adults are sexually dimorphic. Females are of a heavier build with a shorter and broader head and become noticeably swollen with eggs during the breeding season. The cloaca of the male is noticeably swollen during the breeding season and protrudes to a greater extent than does that of the female throughout the rest of the year. A sudden increase of water volume seems to stimulate breeding even outside of the normal breeding season, especially if fairly cool water is used. Be careful, however, that females do not merely develop eggs and then not lay them when artificial methods such as this are utilized. Retained eggs cause death in a variety of amphibian species, although I have not experi-

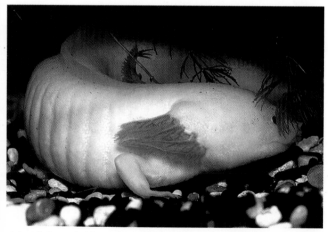

A leucistic axolotl is white, but has branching reddish gills.

enced that happening with axolotls. They seem to always lay once eggs are developed. There is evidence that breeding males secrete pheromones from the cloaca to attract females, who butt the male with their snout about the cloacal region. The male releases the spermatophore, which is pyramidal in shape, and then leads the female, who continues to maintain snout contact with his cloaca, over the spermatophore. Females have been observed to pick up several spermatophores during the night. Eggs are attached to water plants or any other substrate within the tank. Plants make a more suitable site for laying because it is easier to remove them from the aquarium. Axolotls are ravenous consumers of their own eggs if left in the same tank. At temperatures of 55 to 60°F (11.5–14°C), eggs will hatch within two to three weeks. I generally incubate them with a mild aeration, just enough to keep the eggs slightly moving. Eggs laid on plants and on floating objects seem to have a higher hatch rate than do those laid along the bottom of the aquarium, so be sure to provide suitable sites for your females.

Larvae: Larvae begin feeding about one day after hatching, the first day being spent motionless on the bottom of the tank. Newly hatched brine shrimp are the most easily handled food, but very finely chopped blackworms (use a razor blade) are accepted. Larvae will also feed upon each other if not given plenty of room and lots of cover. Bare-bottom tanks are best for raising the larvae. I have not had any luck in switching the larva to dry food until they are about 2 inches (5 cm) long. At this point they will begin to take sinking trout chow and eventually will learn to swim to the surface for floating chow. This greatly simplifies cleaning. As discussed previously, trout chow with occasional supplementation of earthworms, blackworms, and small fish seems to provide an excellent diet for

A larval axolotl, Ambystoma mexicanum.

these animals. I have raised several generations on the trout chow based diet. When feeding blackworms be aware that the young will attempt to engulf large balls of these worms, and may choke. Even chopped blackworms seem to congregate into small balls. While not overly aggressive toward each other when uncrowded, the feeding of live food seems to stimulate a near frenzy and animals will routinely grab the gills and toes of their tank-mates. Generally these grow back without problems, but a treatment with Stresscoat or Novaqua is recommended to prevent infection.

The attractively patterned marbled salamander, Ambystoma opacum, *spends most of its life underground.*

Marbled Salamander
(Ambystoma opacum)

Range and habitat: The marbled salamander ranges from southern New England to northern Florida, and west to southern Illinois, eastern Oklahoma and eastern Texas. It is said that there are disjunct populations along the southern perimeter of Lake Michigan. The marbled salamander is a terrestrial creature as an adult and inhabits woodlands and to a lesser extent, fields and even moist, sandy areas. One can live for many years within their habitat and not know of their existence. This is true of most salamanders (and of the mole salamanders in particular), but even more so for the marbled salamander. Even during the breeding season, it does not form large aggregations and does not leave the telltale aquatic eggs.

Description: The marbled salamander is a member of the family Ambystomatidae, the mole salamanders. True to the family name, this attractively patterned creature spends most of its life underground, either in burrows of its own making or sheltering within those made by rodents or invertebrates. It is a small but strikingly marked creature. The adult size is 3½ to 4½ inches (9–11 cm), and occasionally slightly longer. The background of the animal is black, and it is marked with cross-bands, often in an hourglass shape, along the entire body. These are white or grayish—generally whiter on the male and grayer on the female—and they contrast quite sharply with the animal's jet black background. Like the others in its family, it is sturdily built, and gives the appearance of being larger because of its stoutness.

Care: This animal makes a fairly hardy although secretive captive. In the terrarium it will utilize the same hideaway or burrow for years, only emerging at night and never wandering far from the entrance. Well-habituated individuals can be induced to feed during the day and in your presence if care is taken and the process is gone about very slowly and carefully. Adults relish small earthworms, blackworms, ¼ to ½ inch crickets (6–13mm), waxworms and other such small invertebrates as may be collected. As adults they do not require a water dish, although an easily exited one can be provided for safety.

Sphagnum moss forms a good substrate. These salamanders will burrow deeper if the top layers dry out. A more permanent terrarium can be fashioned from soil, dead leaves, peat moss, and sphagnum. If allowed to form permanent burrow systems, a variety of interesting behaviors might be observed. I would urge those interested in these creatures to house them in very deep aquariums so that the depth and extent of their burrowing can be observed and the effects of dryness on the inhabitants can be monitored. One way to do this would be to block the back of the terrarium so that all burrowing would be confined to the area along the front glass or, alternatively, to cover the glass with black paper to induce the animal to burrow alongside the glass. Remove the paper for observation.

Breeding: This salamander follows a very unique lifestyle in terms of its breeding behavior. The eggs are laid in the fall (in contrast to all the other members of its family) and they are laid on land (also a unique characteristic). The female remains with the eggs in a small depression, generally under some sort of cover. The nest is situated along the sides of a temporary pool. While dry at the time of egg-laying, the depression will fill with water at least to the level of the eggs during a winter thaw or the spring rains. The eggs hatch at that time, in mid winter or early spring, and the larvae begin feeding immediately on fairy shrimp or other small invertebrates that are active even during the cold months. Inducing breeding in captivity requires a winter cooling period (which would seem to be beneficial to the animal's health in general) and a simulation of the very specific breeding habitat utilized by the species. If one is fortunate enough to obtain fertile eggs, they should be left with the female for approximately 6 weeks to 2 months, at which time water should be added until it reaches the level of the eggs. Hatching should occur quickly at that time. Detailed observations would be most interesting and useful to others.

Larvae: The larvae are predisposed to fast growth and require a good deal of food. Upon hatching, they are only about ½ inch (13 mm) long and require newly hatched brine shrimp, infusoria, and very finely chopped blackworms. As they mature, blackworms can form the basis of the diet, supplemented occasionally with chopped tiny earthworms. The larvae will prey upon each other, unless given plenty of room and lots of cover or housed separately. They are about 2.4 to 3.2 inches (6–8 cm) long when they transform into the land-dwelling form, and become sexually mature when just over one year old. By the time late March rolls around and most of the other salamanders are beginning to hatch, the marbled salamanders have been feeding for several weeks and, it is theorized, are now large enough to consume their smaller relatives. This bounty of high-protein food jumpstarts their growth and they are able to metamorphose and leave the pond before it dries up in mid- to late summer. I am not quite sure when they hatch in southern New York State, but those that are swimming about in mid-March transform to adults by mid-to late July. This unique breeding pattern predisposes the marbled salamander to special problems as developers invade its habitat. For one thing, this breeding strategy requires a small temporary pool that is dry in the fall and fills with water in mid- to late winter or early spring. A further problem is that a small dry depression is generally not regarded as important wildlife habitat, even if someone were inclined to check before beginning construction. Also, since the pools are generally very small and many are along roadways or in the catch basins in poorly drained soils, their water volume is apt to be polluted rapidly by runoff and pesticides used in the surrounding areas. As the water levels drop in June and July, pollutants are concentrated and more likely to kill the creatures living therein. The marbled salamander is increasingly being regarded as a species of special concern within its range and, hopefully, will be protected in the near future.

Tiger Salamander
(Ambystoma tigrinum)

Range and habitat: This member of the family *Ambystomatidae* (the mole salamanders), is the largest land-dwelling species in North America. The record length for the eastern race, which is *A. t. tigrinum,* is 13 inches (33 cm). It also has the greatest range of any North American salamander, occurring from extreme southeastern Alaska east to the southern part of Labrador and south throughout the entire United States to the southern edge of the Mexican Plateau. While some of the discussion concerning other members of the family such as the spotted salamander, (*Ambystoma maculatum*) and the marbled salamander, *Ambystoma opacum,* can be applied to the tiger salamander, this animal is quite unique in many ways and can make a long-lived and interesting captive. Many populations, however, are protected, including those occurring in New York State, where

The tiger salamander, Ambystoma tigrinum, *is the largest land-dwelling species in the United States.*

the animal is found only in the pine barrens areas of Long Island. They require fishless ponds to breed, as the eggs have no protection against predation by fish. Introduction of sport or pet fish (such as goldfish) to their breeding ponds is causing a severe reduction in population numbers, as is the development and acidification of these areas. As with many other salamanders, the breeding pools are often temporary and dry up by mid-summer and are often overlooked as suitable habitat for creatures by those who might be checking into such things before an area is slated for development. Fully metamorphosed adults lead a terrestrial existence and, depending upon where in the country they are found, may inhabit forests, grasslands, or marshy areas. One general requirement seems to be soil in which they are able to burrow or in which the burrows of other species of animals might be utilized. While they are well suited for terrestrial existence in terms of their skin consistency and thickness, they do need to be able to go underground in order to seek the proper humidity levels. During dry periods, large num-

bers of tiger salamanders have been found lying in piles beneath suitable cover or underground. Laboratory tests have shown that single individuals lose water more rapidly than those that are piled on top of each other. It thus appears that this is an adaptation to survive dry periods by preventing water loss. Tadpoles of the African bullfrog, *Pyxicephalus adspersus* have been observed to follow a similar strategy. When their ponds dry up they clump together and although the hot sun may kill several on top, those underneath remain moist and may survive until the rains come.

Description: The adult tiger salamander is a thick-bodied creature. Coloration, generally yellow blotches, spots, or bars against a jet black background, is quite stunning. Occasionally, the blotches and spots are a goldish to olive green in color. The size, shape, quantity, and position of the blotches vary among individuals within a population and among populations. Often it is possible to determine the origin of an animal by its general background coloration and spotting pattern, although this issue is confused by the fact that larvae are widely introduced throughout the United States. These introductions are caused most often by fishermen releasing larvae that they have been using for fish bait. While a shocking practice to those interested in amphibians, it is fairly common in certain parts of the country to collect large quantities of larvae as the breeding pools begin to dry and before the animals have transformed into the adult phase and to sell them to fishermen. Sometimes these animals are shipped to other states and are released or escape from the hook and survive, interbreeding with local populations or establishing new populations. This greatly confuses the issue of subspecies classification and range determination. This practice is illegal in areas where the animal is protected, such as New York. In fact, disturbance of breeding habitat is also prohibited in New York. While a noble idea, protection of breeding ponds does not necessarily ensure the species survival. The terrestrial adults seem to wander widely and probably require a good deal of space in which to live as well as a safe corridor to return to the pond. Generally, only the pond and the area about 75 feet (22 m) from its edges are protected, which is most likely not enough habitat to support adult populations of this large animal. The tiger salamander's head, which is large and broad, houses a mouth with a wide gape. It is capable of taking quite large prey, up to the size of a small mouse. The eyes are small and are located near the corners of the mouth. There are tubercles at the bottom of the feet and hands that seem to assist in digging.

A larval tiger salamander.

Care: As both larva and adults, tiger salamanders are voracious feeders and adults will tend to get obese in captivity if given all they can eat. Captive tiger salamanders exhibit an unusual degree of alertness and boldness. They will completely abandon their secretive ways, prowling about in the daytime when hungry. I have observed them on many instances to leave their shelters and walk over to the glass when I approach the terrarium. When I open the top of the tank, they look up and try to climb the glass in anticipation of food. Most feed readily from the hand. Those that do not see you approach can often be brought out of hiding by a slight tapping on the glass. If fed after this they will soon make the association and respond each time. Because of their large size, it is easy to provide a well-balanced diet. While I have on rare occasions observed animals to feed upon dead insects, thereby indicating

that they may possibly use their sense of smell, in general they seem to feed on live prey only. Earthworms, crickets, and waxworms can make up the bulk of the diet, but other insects can be added as available. In the wild they also have been observed to prey upon other amphibians and may thus have some form of protection against the skin toxins of smaller salamanders. I would not experiment in captivity with this, however. I have once observed one grab a small bullfrog, immediately release it, and then rub its snout along the soil, possibly indicating that it was irritated by secretions from the bullfrog's skin. Tiger salamanders will readily consume pink mice and perhaps in the wild they occasionally stumble upon a field mouse nest and consume the young. However, such animals would most certainly not form a major part of their diet and I would avoid giving them too many in captivity. Recent evidence has indicated that carnivorous lizards and perhaps salamanders that are fed too many vertebrates can develop liver problems. Opaque corneas seem to be an indication that the animal is receiving too much in the way of vertebrate prey. While this research is still in the early stages, I think it would be safer to err on the side of caution and provide a diet consisting mainly of invertebrates. Adult tiger salamanders can be housed in a woodland terrarium. If the soil is used, semipermanent burrows will be dug and utilized. Please bear in mind that these are large animals with big appetites and they produce copious amounts of waste products; therefore, complete cleaning of the terrarium is the rule. This is very hard to accomplish in a complicated, stable set up. Damp sphagnum is generally a better alternative.

Breeding: Tiger salamanders breed quite early in the year and during very cold weather, even for a salamander. On Long Island in New York they have been observed to move from their terrestrial hibernation sites to the breeding ponds during warm spells in January, and eggs have been found in February. This is still well within the winter season, and snows and complete refreezing of the ponds often occur after egg laying. Individuals might travel some distance from their usual habitat to the breeding ponds. Such migrations generally occur at night during damp weather or during late winter rains. This is often the only time that these animals give evidence of their presence. During the remainder of the year they shelter deep within self-dug burrows or those made by small mammals. A long period of wet weather may bring them to the surface on occasion, but they are not often encountered even by those searching for them. Breeding takes place in the water. Generally, many males surround one or two females. To breed successfully, males need to separate a female from the group of

salamanders. This is done by repeated head butts to the female's side. A female ready to mate will allow the male to push her away from the group, often seemingly balanced upon his snout. Once she has been separated from the other males, the successful male will head-butt the female's cloaca region and then walk before her while brushing her snout with his tail. If all goes well, the female will follow the male, pushing against his cloaca with her snout, at which point he will release the sperm package, or spermatophore. The spermatophore is taken into the female's cloaca by the cloacal lips, thereby completing the mating process and allowing for internal fertilization. Egg laying generally begins within a few hours. The eggs may number from 20 to over 100 within each gelatinous mass. The entire mass is attached to broken twigs, sticks, or aquatic vegetation. Many such clusters are laid over the course of the next day or so, with especially large females laying up to 5,000 eggs. Typical clutches might be 1,000 to 3,000.

Larvae: Despite the huge numbers of eggs laid, very few survive to reproductive size as the larvae are an important source of food for each other and for other creatures within the pond. Studies have indicated that tiger salamander larvae prefer to prey upon nonrelated animals, exhibiting a type of kin recognition. In those parts of the range where the breeding ponds dry up and disappear, certain members of the population have been observed to develop broader heads and larger teeth than other larvae. These animals then begin feeding ravenously on the other larvae and consequently grow quicker than those animals feeding on the more typical diet of small invertebrates. Because their rapid growth allows for early transformation, these more aggressive larvae are able to enter the land phase before the pond dries up. A dried pond during the larval stage would cause the death of the animals, which have gills for breathing and skin that is not adapted to surviving on land. The mechanics of this change to a highly aggressive, structurally different larvae are not completely understood at this time. In captivity, I have observed large larvae to go into rapid development when the water level is lowered. Removing about ⅛ to ¼ of the water each day caused an almost immediate onset of the loss of gills and the transformation to adult form. Whether this would occur with all populations or whether there are animals specially adapted to this process is not known at this time. If left with a good deal of water and adequate food, and in uncrowded conditions, certain larvae will grow to quite large sizes, 8 to 10 inches (20.3–25.4 cm), and not exhibit signs of transformation for several years. Again, some populations might be adapted to this because of the habitats in which they occur. I am uncertain of the origins of the animals in which I have seen this occur, so I cannot draw any conclusions. Certain populations of tiger salamanders, especially in the Pacific Northwest and in the arid areas of their range in Mexico, exhibit neoteny, and breed in the larval form. The adult terrestrial stage is completely lacking. Such large "mature larvae" may be 11 inches (30 cm) in length. Larvae often transform within three to four months, by fall of the year in which they were hatched.

Spotted Salamander
(Ambystoma maculatum)

Range and habitat: This member of the mole salamander family, or the Ambystomatidae, is in the same genus as the previously discussed tiger salamander, *Ambystoma tigrinum*. In many ways it follows a similar life cycle. It is found throughout eastern North America and ranges north to south-central Ontario, south to Georgia, and west to eastern Texas. It appears to be absent from large portions of southern New Jersey and other parts of the coastal plain such as the Delmarva Peninsula. The adult habitat is generally forested and in the proximity of the breeding pond. While they may occasionally be found under logs or within rotting logs, usually the adults are underground in self-dug burrows or those that have been abandoned by small mammals.

Description: The spotted salamander is a stoutly built creature, but does not grow nearly as large as the tiger salamander. Most animals are 5 to 7 inches long (12.7–17.7 cm) with the record being 9¼ inches (24.8 cm). Adults are generally jet black or bluish black with rows of irregular yellow or occasionally orange spots. Rare individuals lack spots altogether, and some are heavily spotted. In common with other members of their genus, they are rarely observed outside of the short breeding season.

Care: The spotted salamander will feed upon blackworms, earthworms, waxworms, small crickets, and other invertebrates. Habituated animals will become fairly used to being fed during the daytime, but they generally do not leave their shelters and actively seek food as do their larger relatives, the tiger salamanders. They are more secretive creatures and are best observed with as little disturbance as possible. Adults do not utilize water except for breeding, although a shallow water dish for emergency measures would certainly do no harm as long as the animals can exit it.

Breeding: In southern New York I have observed this salamander breeding generally around the third week of March. At this time the water is quite

The spotted salamander, Ambystoma maculatum, *is found throughout eastern North America.*

cold and there is occasionally still snow on the ground. I have spoken with people who have observed breeding migrations of spotted salamanders actually cross the snow to reach their breeding ponds. The sexes appear to arrive at the ponds at separate times, the males first and the females with the next warming rain. For those of you familiar with the

An unspotted specimen of Ambystoma maculatum.

times at which frogs breed (which is easier to determine than salamanders because of their vocalizations) I have found on Long Island and in Westchester County, New York that spotted salamanders often breed in ponds during the same weeks in March as do the spring peepers, *Pseudacris crucifer* and wood frogs, *Rana sylvatica*. Many spotted salamanders are killed by cars during the breeding migration, and others fall into drainage sumps or ditches where they eventually perish. If you know of a spotted salamander breeding pond, you might look into organizing a local nature center to help patrol the area during the nights on which they breed. This has been done with great success in some places and it has caused substantial reductions in the number of road killed and trapped animals. Because the breeding occurs within a very short period of time, this is an example of something that can be done with a minimum time expenditure and that has a real chance of helping the salamanders. A little bit of observation and talks with local people will give you a time frame within which to expect the breeding to occur.

As with the tiger salamander, captive breeding requires a winter cooling period, the temperature of which will vary depending upon the animal's range.

Larvae: If too long a time passes between the time the males arrive in the pond and the next rain that brings the females, males may leave the pond and breeding may not occur that year. This is one of the reasons why it is difficult to assess amphibian populations. The year may appear prime for salamander breeding, with high water levels and frequent rains, but if the timing of the rains is not right, there may be no larvae produced at all that year. This complicates the issue of whether or not certain populations are disappearing or just following normal cycles. The larval stage and the egg-laying process is similar to that described for the tiger salamander. The larvae are, of course, much smaller, hatching out at ½ inch (1–3 cm) in size. Metamorphosis always occurs within the same summer at a size of about 2.4 inches (6 cm). Generally the pools in which spotted salamanders breed are temporary, which is one reason for the rapid larval development.

Plethodontidae

Dusky Salamander
(Desmognathus fuscus)

There are seven to ten species of dusky salamanders, all belonging to the family Plethodontidae, the lungless salamanders. Several of the species have been broken down into sub-species, and the status of others is unclear, especially where ranges overlap.

Range and habitat: The dusky salamanders have reached their greatest diversity in the Appalachian Mountains of the eastern United States. The northern dusky salamander ranges south to Florida and as far west as Texas. The unique features of the dusky salamanders have led some taxonomists to place them in the sub-family Desmognathinae, along with the genus *Leurognathus* and *Phaeognathus.* The northern dusky salamander and several others are mainly confined to wet areas along small flowing creeks and streams. They live a semiaquatic lifestyle, occasionally entering the water, but are generally found in the very wet areas right along the shore, usually under rocks. I have only encountered them under rocks where some water had collected. Generally, dusky salamanders inhabit clear, cool flowing waters although *Desmognathus auriculatus* is found

A larval spotted salamander.

near stagnant ponds. An interesting characteristic of this subfamily is that several species are highly terrestrial, although always found in moist locations, and lack an aquatic larval stage. One of these is known as the pygmy salamander, *Desmognathus wrighti,* which is found only in the region of the border of Virginia, Tennessee, and North Carolina. *D. aeneus* also lays eggs from which terrestrial larvae hatch. The following remarks refer to

The dusky salamander, Desmognathus fuscus, *lacks lungs and gills. All respiration occurs through the skin.*

the northern dusky salamander, although most can be applied to the other species.

Description: Because dusky salamanders lack lungs and gills, all respiration is through the skin; a moist environment, therefore, is a must. When disturbed, they are quite agile, and run remarkably fast for a salamander. Their rear legs are much more heavily built than the front, and they seem to actually leave the land when running. They will enter water when pursued, and are agile swimmers despite the lack of a tail specially adapted for swimming. The northern dusky salamander is one of the largest species, occasionally reaching 7.2 inches (18 cm). *Desmognathus aeneus* is the smallest, maturing at 1.6 inches (4 cm) and rarely exceeding 2.5 inches (6 cm). One characteristic of the subfamily is that they open their mouths by raising the upper jaw. They are variable in coloration, even among the same species, but most are some shade of brown with a lighter stripe down the center. There is usually a light band from the eye to the corner of the mouth. *Desmognathus quadramaculatus*, known as the black-bellied salamander, occasionally reaches 8.4 inches (21 cm) and lives a largely aquatic life-style as an adult, in contrast to most of the other species.

Care: Temperature requirements may be different, depending on the natural range of the animal in question, and of course care of larva will change depending on whether or not the larva are aquatic or terrestrial. The northern dusky salamander should be kept in a moist terrarium with a water section. The highest temperature that they will tolerate is about 65°F (18°C). A basement is an ideal location for a terrarium housing this animal. The water section should have a circulating pump. Peat moss, sphagnum moss, and carpet moss should form the land section, where hiding spots such as rocks and tree bark should be located.

Breeding: If one wishes to breed this species, the individuals should be subjected to a hibernation period. The last meal should be about ten days before hibernation, at which time the temperature should slowly be lowered to about 43°F (6°C). The dusky salamander should be overwintered in very wet sphagnum moss, or shallow water covered by sphagnum. They will move about slightly during hibernation but not require food. As with many lungless salamanders, the male initiates a sort of courtship dance, wherein he touches the female on the snout with his head and curls his body around her. Male dusky salamanders possess a submandibular gland in the lower jaw. This is rubbed back and forth over the female's head and dorsal surface. The secretions that are exuded seem to stimulate the female into readiness to mate. The female, who follows the male as he walks away, has been seen to rub his tail with her front leg. At this point, he releases a spermatophore, which she picks up and takes into her cloaca. The female deposits 10 to 40 eggs about six to eight weeks later in a secluded wet area, usually below or within some sort of shelter such as a log. The eggs clump together, and she wraps her

A larval dusky salamander.

body around them. Some salamanders that guard eggs have been seen to attack and eat or drive off potentially predatory invertebrates, so one would imagine this would hold true for the dusky salamander as well. The female's body wrapped around the eggs may also prevent desiccation. It is not known whether the female eats during this period, although they have been seen to leave the clutch for short periods of time.

Larvae: Hatching is in four to five weeks, and the larvae are approximately ½ inch (13 mm) long when they emerge from the eggs. They remain in the sheltered area of the nest cavity for ten days to two weeks, then move to the water where external gills develop. As you may know, this is an unusual twist on salamander development. Larvae transform into the terrestrial adult form in seven to ten months, depending on range and temperature. Sexual maturity is believed to be reached in three years, although this may vary in the captive situation. As is typical for most terrestrial salamanders, adults will feed upon small earthworms, small slugs, tiny insects, and blackworms. Terrestrial larva will take the same food but in much smaller sizes. Pinhead crickets, ten day old crickets, and aphids as well as chopped blackworms are about the only items newly hatched dusky salamanders can handle.

Green Salamander
(Aneides aeneus)

Range: The green salamander is the only member of the genus that occurs in the eastern United States, and is restricted to the area of the Appalachian Mountains. The other three members of the genus occur in the Pacific Northwest and one ranges south into New Mexico. Within the Appalachian region, this animal occurs in southwestern Pennsylvania, western Maryland, from southern Ohio to central Alabama, and in a small area of northeastern Mississippi. There is also apparently a disjunct population in southwestern North Carolina and possibly, since it is a secretive animal and difficult to study, neighboring areas in other states.

Description: This animal is fairly easy to recognize as it is the only North American species that is actually green in color. The background color is mottled with darker blotches that resemble patches of lichen. One can imagine that this provides excellent camouflage in the rocky habitat in which this animal occurs. The four species within the genus *Aneides* are referred to as climbing salamanders or tree salamanders. The genus is classified within the family Plethodontidae. These salamanders lack gills and lungs, and therefore require an extremely moist habitat to facilitate cutaneous respiration. The green salamander has squared off toe tips, which may assist in climbing. Generally, it prefers regions where there are a great many narrow rock crevices into which it can secure itself to prevent desiccation and to escape the notice of predators. It has occasionally been recorded as inhabiting holes in trees or the moist areas under loose bark on tree trunks, but it seems more typically found among rock piles than are the other three species.

Care: Flat rocks such as shale over a damp substrate of sphagnum moss make an ideal captive habitat for the species. Bear in mind that this animal is a particularly adept climber, adapted to squeezing into and through small cracks; therefore, take care in securing the top of the green salamander's terrarium. Standing water is not necessary, but the tank should be very damp. Perhaps a shallow water bowl or a reservoir of water below the sphagnum moss might be kept as a

Green, with darker patches that resemble lichens, Aneides aeneus, *the green salamander, is native to the eastern United States.*

safety precaution. Since it will often choose to shelter within the rock crevices as opposed to within the moss, these should be wet daily, and should be checked to be sure that moisture is accumulating between the rock slabs. Rock does not hold water as does moss, so it is a little more difficult to keep this animal moist than it might be for other terrestrial salamanders. You might wedge some moss between the rock slabs to help keep up moisture levels within these retreats. As the green salamander only grows to 3 to 5 inches (7.2–12 cm) upon maturity, only small food items are accepted, including ¼-inch (6 mm) crickets, small chopped earthworms, blackworms, and tiny waxworms. Ideally, these should be supplemented with tiny insects collected by sweeping a net through tall grass or by searching under decaying logs.

Breeding: As with many strictly land-dwelling salamanders, the green salamander (and the others within the genus) lay eggs on land, and the eggs hatch into small, fully developed salamanders. There is no aquatic larval stage. The eggs of the green salamander generally hatch in the fall, having been laid the previous spring. The eggs are stalked, and there are generally 10 to 20 of them, depending upon the species. They are guarded by the female, who apparently drives off egg predators. Generally, they are laid within a small damp crevice in wood or rock, where there is usually space only for the eggs and the female. Those working with the green salamanders would do well to obtain exact locality data for their specimens. In most areas of their range, a somewhat cooler winter period would probably be required to stimulate reproduction. Those in the northern parts of the range would almost certainly require this. The species from the West Coast would seem to require less of a chill, and those in New Mexico might require a different regimen all together (such as a dry season). Animals in New Mexico as well as those that occur in California and Oregon are actually found in the mountains and so are not exposed to temperatures as warm as one might imagine.

Other species: The other five species within the genus are the clouded salamander, *Aneides ferreus,* the black salamander, *Aneides flavipunctatus,* the Sacramento Mountain salamander, *Aneides hardyi*, and the arboreal salamander, *Aneides lugubris.* The clouded salamander is found in western Oregon and northern California. It somewhat resembles the green in that it has a marbled pattern against the dark background, but it is much more of a gray and black combination as opposed to the green. The black salamander is found along the coast of California and Oregon, mainly in the mountains, and is black with tiny yellow spots. The Sacramento Mountain salamander is restricted to the mountains bearing its name in New Mexico. The arboreal salamander is found in California and into Baja California, Mexico. It is brown with yellowish dots.

Red-backed Salamander
(Plethodon cinereus)

This tiny creature, a member of the family Plethodontidae, or lungless salamanders, relies entirely on oxygen transfer through its skin for respiration. It is an amazing creature in its habits, its adaptations, and its importance in the ecosystem. The red-backed salamander is considered the most terrestrial of all salamanders.

Range and habitat: This salamander has evolved a lifestyle that is completely independent of standing water, although it does require moisture to facilitate the transfer of oxygen through the skin. It has a wide range, occurring from southern Quebec to Minnesota, and south to North Carolina and Missouri. Within parts of its range, studies have found it to be the most abundant of all vertebrates. Its biomass, or the weight of all of the individuals within a certain area, has been estimated to be equal to or greater than that of all the reptiles, amphibians, birds, and mammals in the ecosystem combined. This figure is made more amazing by the fact that these creatures are only 2 to 4 inches (5–10 cm) in length when full grown and very thinly built. Especially in the eastern United States, populations are said to reach over 1,000 per acre. Their importance to the overall functioning of the ecosystem can thus not be overstressed. It is, therefore, quite alarming that they are becoming harder to find in many areas. I have observed this by casual studies, and others have documented the fact that populations are dropping. Laboratory tests have indicated that red-backed salamanders will move away from substrates that have become

Plethodon cinereus, *the red-backed salamander, is completely independent of standing water—although a moist environment is essential for the transfer of oxygen and carbon dioxide through its skin.*

acidified. This may be one of the chief causes of their disappearance in the Northeast. Acid rain will change the chemical composition of the soil and the dead leaves in which they live, causing them to seek other areas. Migrations to avoid acid conditions generally result in high losses to the populations, especially among animals that occupy a specific territory throughout their lives, as do red-backed salamanders. Also, if an area of the habitat is affected by acid rain, it is extremely unlikely that these animals can travel far enough to find better habitat. Animals confined to acidic substrates in the laboratory weaken and die.

Adult red-backed salamanders most likely do not enter standing water at all. They regulate moisture by their habitat choice or, more specifically, their choice of location within the habitat. These animals are fairly tolerant of the cold and may be seen moving about under logs even on warm days in December in New York. They can be found on the surface under rocks,

A lead-backed specimen of Plethodon cinereus.

logs, and dead leaves when there is sufficient moisture, or else they are deeper within the soil layer.

Description: The red-backed salamander is extremely variable in coloration, both throughout its range and among individuals within the same habitat. Most commonly, a red or reddish dorsal stripe down the center of the back is exhibited. Other specimens have light gray stripes, and some have dark gray, or even black backs. These are generally referred to as lead-backed salamanders, but they are the same species as the red-backed. The abdomen is generally marbled or flecked with black and white or black and yellow. The two color phases interbreed, producing a wide spectrum of variations.

Red-backed salamanders seem to possess strong skin toxins that discourage many predators. In the presence of a potential predator, the animal elevates and lashes its tail back and forth. Red-backed salamanders will also drop the tail, which remains wiggling for some time, to distract predators so that the salamander might make its escape. The lost tail portion is regenerated. Salamanders grasped in the jaws of small snakes such as the brown snake, *Storeria*

dekayi, will lash about with their tail, turn, and bite at the snake. This has been shown to cause the release of the otherwise doomed animal.

Care: Even fully grown adults are incapable of taking anything but quite small prey. One-quarter inch (6 mm) crickets, blackworms, and finely chopped, tiny earthworms can form the basis of the diet. Because of their small size, complex, well-planted terrariums can be created. However, despite their size, these animals should be given as much room as possible in captivity so that natural patterns of territoriality might be observed. If one can establish a small group within a very large terrarium, such behavior should soon be evident. Red-backed salamanders produce only small amounts of waste products and seem to pile feces at the edges of their territory. If this is observed, cleaning should be regulated so as to leave a bit of this to help preserve natural behaviors among mating animals. Also, because they are so territorial, constant habitat disturbance such as emptying of the whole tank, which is the rule for many other salamanders, might throw off their behavior and feeding. For this reason a very large, well-planted terrarium with a few animals, which need not be broken down and completely cleaned, is ideal. When cleaning is done, efforts should be made to replace structures within the terrarium in exactly the same way as they were so that the animals do not have to be accustomed to new surroundings. In this way, normal behaviors and breeding might occur.

Breeding: The red-backed salamander has been shown to be extremely territorial. Individuals appear to know their territory very well and are able to return to it based mostly on olfactory cues. Males apparently mark their territory with small piles of fecal material, and females have been observed to investigate these piles, apparently using the scent of the feces to determine the diet of the male. Choice of a mate is made partially based upon this assessment. The males with a high-quality diet would most likely be chosen over those with a poorer diet. There is evidence that male territories are defended.

At first glance the red-backed salamander is a tiny and apparently relatively simple creature. Its courtship behaviors, however, are so complex that they cannot help but remind us of all the fascinating things we can observe and learn about even the smallest of animals. After the female has made the complex determination, based on scent, of which male is the most suitable prospect as a mate, she will enter his territory, whereupon he will push her with his snout and nip at her. He then sequentially raises and lowers each leg in front of her while pushing his snout against her throat region and moving below her. The animals then walk together with body and tail in contact, the male on the bottom, the female above. At some point he deposits a spermatophore. The spermatophore, as with other salamanders, is taken up by the cloacal lips and internal fertilization occurs. Only three to eleven individual eggs are laid—far fewer than most species; but constant parental care ensures a fairly high hatch rate. They are generally laid in a small cave or depression below a rock or log and are attached to the ceiling of the depression. The female remains within the small cave, curled up below the eggs. Possibly her body provides moisture for the development of the eggs. Females have also been observed to bite at small creatures that might possibly feed upon the eggs. It is not certain whether or not the female actually eats during this period. There is some evidence that the female will remove

An "intermediate phase" red-backed salamander.

eggs that have developed fungus, presumably to prevent the fungus from spreading to the rest of the clutch.

Part of this species' success, in terms of numbers, is due to the fact that it maintains regular territories with which it is completely familiar and also because of its strategy of breeding on land within that territory. Breeding migrations to ponds from a land habitat are a tremendous source of mortality to adult salamanders. This is true even in undisturbed habitats because of sudden changes in weather, and because the animals are up on the surface moving about and exposed to predators. In developed areas, the mortality is all the more higher due to road kill and because the animals fall into various excavations.

Captive breeding might occur if a cooling winter period were established along with lower light levels.

Larvae: In contrast to many salamanders, the young hatch out as perfectly formed miniatures of the adult. They do have tiny external gills that are absorbed within a few days. In

A young northern red salamander, Pseudotriton ruber ruber, *is one of the most brilliantly colored of all salamander species.*

Northern Red Salamander
(Pseudotriton ruber ruber)

Range and habitat: The northern red salamander ranges from southern New York and Ohio to northern Alabama. The red salamander's activities are restricted almost entirely to the very wet areas along the banks of running streams. It is very specific in this regard, never being found near stagnant water. Because it requires clean, cool, flowing water, it is, or soon will be, in danger throughout much of its range. It seems even more sensitive to water quality and temperature than other salamanders. It is a member of the family Plethodontidae, and, lacking gills and lungs, must confine its activities to cool, wet areas in order to allow for respiration through the skin.

Description: Most red salamanders are about 5 inches (12.7 cm) long, although specimens slightly in excess of 7 inches (17.8 cm) have been found. A young northern red salamander is one of the most spectacularly colored of all salamanders. The brilliant red background is highlighted by jet black flecks along the back and the legs. As the animals mature, the red tends to fade, and very old animals are often a dark purple or reddish brown in color.

Care: The captive care of the red salamander presents some problems. I have found them to be quite hardy and long lived once the proper conditions are set up, but they are very strict in their requirements and fail to thrive unless all details of proper care are adhered to. The water must be clean, cool, and dechlorinated. While they are not strictly aquatic, they do tend to spend more time in the water than do other, more terrestrial members of their family. In other words, they don't generally actively swim unless alarmed, but are often found in habitats that are partially submerged

all other respects, the larval stage is completely skipped. Sexual maturity is reached in about 1½ years. Newly hatched young are quite difficult to feed because of their size. If aphids are available, these would form an ideal food source as would pinhead and ten-day crickets.

Subspecies: Several subspecies of the red-backed salamander have been described, although interbreeding along the edges of the range makes identification difficult. The Ouachita red-backed salamander, formerly *Plethodon cinereus serratus,* has recently been given full species status. Now known as the Southern red-backed salamander, *P. serratus,* its dorsal midstripe has saw-toothed edges. Otherwise, the coloration is generally similar to the red-backed salamander. This creature occurs in the mountains of central Arkansas and Oklahoma, western central Louisiana, Georgia, Alabama, Tennessee, and North Carolina.

and where they can maintain contact with water. This being the case, and considering their delicate nature, it might be safer to use bottled water when keeping these animals. While they can be kept in wet sphagnum moss if it is changed frequently, an ideal setup would be a large aquarium with a shallow water section filtered by a submersible filter. The land area can be moss over gravel. Generally, the streams near which these animals are found have gravel bottoms. The gravel will keep the moss from contact with the water, therefore aiding in maintaining cleanliness. If the moss bed is deep enough, the animals seem to make semipermanent burrows. (I have found them in the same locations for weeks on end.) They are fairly shy and extremely secretive. They almost never venture out during the day even after years in captivity. If care is taken, they can be induced to feed at the opening of a favorite hideaway. They have fairly small mouths, so food items must be sized accordingly. They relish blackworms, small earthworms, ¼- to ½-inch (6–13 mm) crickets, and very tiny waxworms. Other soft-bodied insects that may be available could be tried as well.

Breeding: A winter cooling period at 40°F (4°C) seems to be necessary to stimulate reproduction and would most likely assist the animals' over-all health. Considering their tolerance for low temperatures, you might consider using your refrigerator as a hibernation chamber. It is essential that the animal be kept wet during hibernation. The eggs, which are guarded by the female, are laid on land under flat rocks or within damp rotting logs, generally very close to the streams near which the adults live. Depending upon the area of the United States in which the salamander is found, eggs may be laid from fall until spring. The eggs take approximately two months to hatch, and there is often a long larval period, sometimes in excess of two and one half years.

Subspecies: Several subspecies of red salamander have been described. The Blue Ridge red salamander, *Pseudotriton ruber nitidus,* does not grow as large as the northern, reaching only 5 inches (12 cm) in length, and lacks black pigment at the end of the tail. Older animals retain their bright red coloration. (The northern red salamander turns a purplish color as it ages.) The Blue Ridge red salamander has been found at elevations of over 5,000 feet (1,500 m) in the Blue Ridge Mountains of Floyd County, Virginia. The black-chinned red salamander *Pseudotriton ruber schencki,* also occurs in the Blue Ridge Mountains at high elevations; it differs in appearance from the northern red in also being smaller and in having a heavier concentration of black along the chin area. As with other salamanders found at higher elevations, temperature must be kept cool to ensure survival.

Other species: The eastern mud salamander, *Pseudotriton montanus montanus*, is a salamander closely

Pseudotriton montanus montanus, *the eastern mud salamander, is closely related to the northern red salamander.*

The spring salamander, Gyrinophilus porphyriticus, *inhabits cool, wet areas along mountain streams.*

related to the red salamander and similar in appearance. One way to distinguish the two species is that the mud salamander's eye is brown while the red salamander's eye is yellow. The habitats are also different; mud salamanders are generally found, as their name indicates, along the muddy sections of slow-moving creeks and streams. They attempt to dig into the mud when disturbed, and appear to

A larval spring salamander.

make use of crayfish burrows. They can be kept in a manner similar to the red salamander, and are equally as shy and as sensitive to high temperatures. The eggs hatch in about two months and the larval stage may last for nearly three years, depending upon temperature. Sexual maturity occurs during the second year.

Spring Salamander (Gyrinophilus porphyriticus)

Range and habitat: There are two very different species within the genus *Gyrinophilus.* The spring salamander *(Gyrinophilus porphyriticus),* ranges from Quebec and southern Maine to Georgia, Alabama, and Mississippi, and exists as a complex of four subspecies. It follows a semiaquatic lifestyle, and is apparently restricted to the cool, very wet areas along shallow mountain streams. The other member of this genus is the Tennessee cave salamander, *Gyrinophilus palleucus.* This animal is neotenic, that is, always remaining as an aquatic creature with external gills. The Tennessee cave salamander is only found in caves within central and southeastern Tennessee, northern Alabama, and northwestern Georgia. It is protected by law, and as far as I know, captive-bred animals are not available.

Description: The spring salamander is quite variable but always startling in coloration. The background can be salmon, pink, reddish, or orange-yellow, and there are usually black flecks on the dorsal surface. It grows to a length of 7½ inches (19 cm), and is an extremely delicate captive.

Care: Having small mouth parts, the salamander is limited to eating tiny invertebrates. Blackworms and small earthworms could form a basis of its diet, and ¼-inch crickets will also be taken.

Breeding: Mating occurs in the fall and the eggs are laid the following spring and sometimes into summer, depending upon the elevation in which the animal is living. Cool temperatures are required and a winter resting period is necessary to stimulate reproduction.

Subspecies: Several subspecies have been identified, each generally limited to one cave or one cave system within the overall range. Some include the Sinking Cave salamander, *G.p. palleucus,* the Big Mouth Cave salamander, *G.p. necturoides*, and the Berry Cave salamander, *G.p. gulolineatus.* As much of their range and habitat is underground, none have been thoroughly studied.

Salamandridae

Spanish Ribbed Newt
(Pleurodeles waltl)

Range: The Spanish ribbed newt is native to the southwestern portion of the Iberian Peninsula and northwestern Morocco.

Description: This is the largest European newt, reaching a length of 12 inches (30 cm). It is dark olive with blackish spots, although the color varies among populations. The skin appears to have warts in two rows along the dorsal surface. These are actually the barely covered tips of the ribs. These "rib warts" are yellow to reddish. When threatened, the ribbed newt will push the rib tips against the skin, thus elevating the poison glands located there. The tips of the ribs are sharp and occasionally will pierce the skin without harming the newt. The head of the Spanish ribbed newt is more flattened than that of other newts, and the tail is laterally compressed to assist in swimming. The species is mainly aquatic, leaving the water for short periods to rest.

Care: In the terrarium Spanish ribbed newts should be provided with a land area and shallow water with floating

Pleurodeles waltl, *the Spanish ribbed newt, is native to the Iberian Peninsula and northwestern Morocco.*

plants. While I have found them to be generally hardy captives, they do seem to require a hiding place, in contrast to many newts that seem to settle down and become quite bold in captivity. The Spanish ribbed newt rarely leaves its hiding place, except to feed. A small inverted clay flower pot or piece of tree bark seems to suit their needs. They're not particularly strong swimmers despite their size so if filtration is used, care should be taken that the current does not disturb the animals. A thick growth of devil's ivy in shallow water will provide them with a suitable aquatic habitat. They will spend a good deal of time poking about the leaves and root system of the plants searching for food that may have escaped their notice. In the wild state, they remain active throughout the year, and are said to pass dry periods buried in mud below rocks. They are quite voracious feeders, and care should be taken that the gravel on which they are kept is not small enough to be swallowed. Like many aquatic newts, the Spanish ribbed newt will take pelleted food in captivity. I have observed them feeding on Reptomin but not trout chow or dried prawn. Other favorites include small crickets, small earthworms, and blackworms.

Spanish ribbed newts in the breeding embrace (amplexus). The male is seen at the bottom.

Larvae: Larvae hatch within one to two weeks, depending on temperature, and can be raised on chopped blackworms and newly hatched brine shrimp. Others have reported feeding the larvae powdered or flake fish food, but I have not had luck in getting any species to eat much dry food in the first few weeks after hatching.

Other species: There is only one other species in the genus, the Algerian ribbed newt *Pleurodeles poireti*. This animal is smaller than the Spanish ribbed newt, reaching only about 6 inches (15 cm) in length, and is found in northeastern Algeria and northern Tunisia.

Subspecies: One subspecies has been described, *Pleurodeles poireti hagenmulleri*.

**Marbled Newt
(*Triturus marmoratus*)**

Range: The two subspecies of marbled newt are found in southwestern France and the Iberian Peninsula.

Description: Marbled newts can reach a length of 6.4 inches (16 cm), although most are somewhat smaller than that. They differ in color from most of the other members of the genus in that their backs are mottled in an attractive green and black pattern. However, other color combinations, including yellow and brown, have been observed. In common with the other nine species within the genus *Triturus,* the marbled newt enters the water after its winter hibernation period. Tails of both species flatten out a bit to allow for swimming, and those of the male develop to a greater extent as a secondary sex characteristic.

Care: Marbled newts can be kept in a terrestrial set-up during most of the year, and after hibernation moved into an aquatic habitat. My experience with similar animals indicates that this change of terrarium type is the most

Breeding: In certain parts of their range, the Spanish ribbed newt breeds throughout the year, whenever conditions are favorable, (i.e., when water levels are high enough). In captivity, also, reproduction might occur at any time. Reproductively active males develop nuptial pads, which are swollen, roughened areas of skin along the inner sides of the two front legs. During courtship, which occurs in water, the male moves below the female and rubs his head against her throat. In a somewhat unusual courtship move, he grips her forearms from below with his forearms. They may stay in this position for several hours. At some point the male will deposit a small spermatophore near the female's head, and he will then turn and position the female so that she can pick up the spermatophore with her cloaca. The eggs are deposited in clumps on submerged branches, plants, and rocks. Large females have been recorded as laying up to 1000 eggs. Egg laying generally takes place about one month after fertilization.

effective way to stimulate breeding. Warm temperatures are to be strictly avoided. 72°F (22°C) is about the highest that these animals can tolerate. During the winter, they should be given a cool period at which time temperatures should be allowed to drop to between 36 and 46°F (2–8°C). The daylight period should be shortened at this time so that a pattern similar to that of the temperate latitudes in which they live is followed. If you are located within a temperate area, a cool basement in winter would probably prove ideal if the tank can be positioned near a window. The exact light intensity does not seem to be so important as the specific period of light and dark. Blackworms, small chopped earthworms, crickets, waxworms, and small insects make up the adult diet. Larvae can be raised on brine shrimp and finely chopped blackworms. Overwintering should occur in damp moss as opposed to water. Marbled newts, and the larvae in particular, are very sensitive to water quality, so strict attention should be paid to cleanliness in their aquarium.

The marbled newt, Triturus mamoratus, *inhabits southwestern France and the Iberian Peninsula.*

Breeding: Males in breeding condition will check females by smelling the cloacal area to determine their receptivity to breeding advances. Courting males position themselves in front of the female, apparently releasing pheromones designed to stimulate the female to follow the male and pick up the spermatophore. The tip of the male's tail is waved while the spermatophores are being released, possibly to create a current that carries the scent toward the female. The spermatophore is generally deposited after the female makes contact with the male's tail or body with her snout. Courting males seem to manipulate the female's position so that she comes into contact with the spermatophore. Fertilized females lay eggs at various times throughout the next two to three months. Eventually a total of up to 200 eggs may be deposited. Each is laid singly on a water plant, and the tip of the plant's leaf is bent over the egg by the female to form a covering for the individual egg. The easiest way to manage such eggs is to remove the entire plant to a separate aquarium. Eggs left within the adult's aquarium are usually eaten. Hatching occurs at two to three weeks, and the young newts transform by the end of the first summer, about two months after they hatch.

Larvae: The larvae follow the typical newt pattern of development, moving onto moist land as they lose their gills. They can be raised in a damp terrarium with only a small water section until they are two to three years old, at which time sexual maturity occurs and they can breed. While faster growth may occur if the animals are kept active all year, these and most other salamanders should ideally be subjected to a winter period even during their growth years. Keeping them on a natural temperature and light cycle may help to encourage normal breeding when the animals are mature.

Eastern Newt
(Notophthalmus viridescens)

Range: The eastern newts consist of a complex of several subspecies within the family Salamandridae. The widest ranging subspecies is commonly referred to as the red-spotted newt *N.v. viridescens* and its range extends from Canada's Maritime Provinces west to the Great Lakes and south to central Georgia.

Description: This newt, which grows to a size of 4 inches (10 cm) and occasionally longer, is generally found in and around quiet waters supporting a good deal of plant growth. Depending upon the range and upon the subspecies, these animals are dark brown to tan in color with red dots that may be encircled by black. Some subspecies also have broken or continuous red stripes along the dorsal surface. The abdomen is yellow to orange. Adult males develop hind legs that are noticeably stronger and thicker than the front legs and that contain black nuptial pads (thickened hard areas) that enable the male to grasp the female during amplexus. Sexual dimorphism is also evident in the shape of the cloaca, the male's being hemispherical while the female's is cone-shaped and projects slightly.

Care: Since these animals are fairly hardy in captivity and are often readily available from captive-bred stock, I would suggest them both as a "first species" and also as an animal to study in depth. This again is an area where one with a great deal of interest and a bit of experience might be able to make important contributions to our knowledge. The aquatic phase of the eastern newt is perhaps the easiest to maintain at home. Depending upon their range, these animals can be a bit more tolerant of warmer temperatures than other salamanders. An aquarium with an easily accessible land area is ideal. Because they are small animals, they are not destructive to complicated setups. One can create quite an elaborate and attractive habitat containing live plants and dead wood, etc. The land area can be a gravel bank or merely some floating cork bark. In the aquatic adult stage, they do need to come out of the water and rest but do not travel extensively on land and do not feed on land. All food is taken in the water and their food preferences are quite wide. The aquatic adult stage will feed upon nonliving food; Reptomin food sticks and trout chow are good staples. They will also readily consume blackworms, newly born guppies, finely chopped earthworms, and brine shrimp, as well as small insects that are thrown into the water. During the eft, or terrestrial stage, they appear to require live food. Because these animals are fairly small, choices are mostly limited to ¼- to ½-inch (6–13 mm) crickets, black-

The eastern newt, Notophthalmus viridescens. *The widest ranging subspecies,* Notophthalamus v. viridescens *(commonly called the red-spotted newt), is shown here.*

worms, chopped earthworms, and whatever tiny invertebrates might be collected. Although efts have a fairly thick skin and are more suited to a land existence than many salamanders, care must be taken that they do not dry out. Moist retreats should always be available within the terrarium and a low water bowl might be included as a safety device. Efts preparing to enter the aquatic phase will exhibit a color change, generally becoming a bit darker, which serves as a signal to increase the water area so that they may frequent this habitat if necessary.

A pair of eastern newts in amplexus.

Breeding: Amplexus may last for several hours and occurs in shallow quiet ponds in spring or fall, depending upon the range of the animal. The female is grasped about the head and chest region from above and is released when the male deposits a spermatophore that the female then takes up into her cloaca. The 200 to 300 eggs are individually attached to water plants, generally in the spring. Egg incubation lasts from three weeks to two months, again depending upon range. Breeding can be achieved in captivity mainly through temperature manipulation and a change in the light phase that the animals are accustomed to. Northern populations do best if given a winter cooling period of several months. They may be refrigerated as low as 35°F (1.5°C) in very shallow water or damp sphagnum moss. Those from the southern parts of the range would require only a temperature dip to about 50 to 59°F (10–15°C) and the period can be shortened to two weeks. Adults will consume the eggs, so they are best removed after the eggs are laid. Live plants form the best substrate for egg laying, although in the absence of these, females will use sticks, stones, and plastic plants. The eggs should be kept with a very light aeration.

Larvae: The larvae are less than .4 inches (1 cm) in length upon hatching.

Being so tiny, they are not easy to raise. Live prey seems to be essential at first. Newly hatched brine shrimp are perhaps the best starter food. One can experiment with dried foods once the larva begin to feed regularly. Due to the size of the larvae, a bare-bottom tank is best so that the food is not lost between cracks in the gravel. Metamorphosis is dependent upon a variety of things, including water chemistry, temperature, and the character of the surrounding habitat. Certain races or subspecies of the eastern newt remain in the larval form throughout their life, exhibiting neoteny, but this is not the common lifestyle. Generally, the larvae transform into a land-dwelling form at about three months of age and a size of approximately 1.6 inches (4 cm). The eastern newts are fairly unique in their lifestyle. Most salamanders that change habitats during their life exhibit a larval form and an adult form. The eastern newt exhibits three forms. The terrestrial stage is referred to as the eft stage. The eft is an animal that grows to slightly under 4 inches

In the red eft stage, the eastern newt is completely terrestrial.

(9.6 cm), is bright orange or red in color, and has a thicker, more roughened skin than the adult aquatic form. This stage lasts from one to three years. During this time the animals live in moist areas, generally within a forested habitat. They are completely terrestrial, feeding upon small inverte-

brates among the leaf litter and under logs. Their bright coloration is a warning of the powerful skin toxins that these animals possess. I know of several instances of people collecting these brightly colored animals and placing them in terrariums with turtles. In several cases turtles that consumed efts died within one hour. Incidentally, adult animals in the aquatic life stage also appear to contain skin toxins although they are not clothed in the bright warning colors of the eft. At the end of the eft stage, the animal returns to water and takes on the coloration of the adult aquatic phase, greenish brown with red dots or stripes. At this point they are sexually mature and ready to breed. The eft stage is occasionally skipped. Most often this occurs among populations living along the eastern coastal plain of the United States and on Long Island in New York. So we can see that among these animals we have a field ripe for investigation to determine the causes of the variety of lifestyles present. Some populations seem to exhibit the different modes with no apparent rhyme or reason, although of course one is there.

Subspecies: A variety of subspecies (and even species of the eastern newt) are occasionally available. The central newt, *Notophthalmus viridescens louisianensis,* has only tiny red spots (usually lacking black outlines) or may lack spots completely. Most common in the South, it ranges from eastern Texas to Lake Superior. It interbreeds with other subspecies of the red-spotted newt, giving rise to animals with a variety of color patterns and background marking patterns. The eft or land stage is generally skipped, especially in the South. In the southeastern coastal plain the animal often exhibits neoteny, skipping the aquatic adult and the land stage. The Peninsula newt, *Notophthalmus viridescens piaropicola* is limited in range to peninsular Florida, and is

The central newt, Notophthalmus viridescens louisianensis.

found in quiet canals, ponds, and ditches. Almost any semipermanent body of water within the peninsula can be found to contain these animals, although as with all salamanders, they seem to be disappearing from certain areas. The Peninsula newt is much darker, generally, than the red-spotted newt and may appear almost black. The eft stage is rare and neoteny is common. Along the coastal plain in North and South Carolina we find the broken-striped newt, *Notophthalmus viridescens dorsalis.* This small creature is unique in appearance among the newts in that it has a red dorsal lateral stripe bordered with black that is broken in one or two places along the head and body. The red eft stage is generally present. The aquatic adults are found in quiet pools of water and occasionally in the quieter sections of streams.

Other species: An animal fairly similar in appearance to the eastern newt but actually a different species is the striped newt, *Notophthalmus perstriatus.* This animal also has a red lateral dorsal stripe, but the stripe is continuous along the animal's body, breaking only near the head and tail. The black border of the red stripe is also not as dark and as even as the broken striped newt. The striped newt ranges from southern Georgia to northern Florida. The black-spotted newt is also a separate species within the genus. Its Latin name is *Notophthalmus meridionalis.* This animal has large black spots and lacks the red ones. It occurs from south Texas into Mexico and is limited to the moist areas around ponds and swamps. The overall habitat is fairly dry so that the animal's range is discontinuous.

Japanese Fire-bellied Newt (Cynops pyrrhogaster)

Range and habitat: This newt exhibits a largely aquatic lifestyle and ranges in size from 3.6 to 5 inches

The striped newt, Notophthalmus perstriatus.

(9–12 cm). It is a member of the family Salamandridae and is native to eastern China and Japan. The Japanese fire-bellied newt inhabits quiet, standing bodies of water that support heavy plant growth.

Description: The upper surface of this newt is dark brown to jet black and sometimes slightly spotted with red. The abdomen is strikingly patterned in orange or deep red, often with black patches. The bright coloration makes quite a contrast against the dark background and serves to warm potential predators of the powerful skin toxins. Obvious paratoid or poison glands are located along the sides of the head.

The black-spotted newt, Notophthalmus meridionalis.

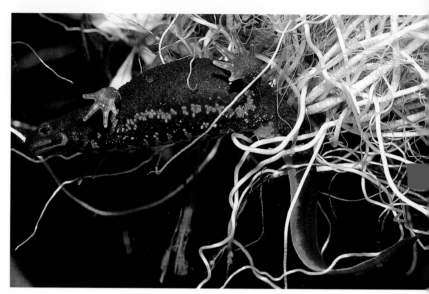

Cynops pyrrhogaster, *the Japanese fire-bellied newt, is native to eastern China and Japan. Its lifestyle is largely aquatic.*

During the breeding season, this animal develops a threadlike extension of the tail tip and the cloaca enlarges.

Care: The Japanese fire-bellied newt makes a fairly hardy terrarium inhabitant. It is mainly found in temperate areas and thus should be overwintered on wet moss at 40 to 50°F (5–10°C) in order to increase the chances of successful breeding. The aquarium for the adults can be composed mainly of water with a small gravel area or floating cork bark for the animals to emerge on. They do not seem to wander extensively on land or to require land-based shelters, being content to float around on cork bark while they rest. They become fairly bold in captivity, readily accepting food from one's fingers. As with many other newts, they rely heavily on scent to find their food and thus will accept pelleted food such as Reptomin food sticks and trout chow. Other favorite food items are chopped earthworms, blackworms, tiny snails, tiny fish, and insects. All food is taken in the water. As their natural habitat is quiet waters, filtration should be mild and not disturb the water column too much. Despite their aquatic nature, they can climb up the sides of glass, so the aquarium needs to be well covered. Cool temperatures are the rule. These animals become fairly stressed at temperatures over 76°F (22°C) and are then subject to fungal infections and skin diseases.

Breeding: Courtship begins in the water with the male butting the female's body with his head. He will swim in front of her to block her progress should she try to move away. The paratoid glands are rubbed along her body and the male's tail is used to fan pheromones, presumably designed to stimulate her into courtship behavior. The spermatophore is picked up by the cloacal lips in typical salamander fashion. Eggs are individually attached to aquatic plants. The tips of a leaf are folded over each egg by the female. The incubation period is short, generally less than 2 weeks.

Larvae: Young follow a typical salamander lifestyle, hatching out as gilled larvae and developing into the semi-aquatic adult form usually within a few months. Sexual maturity is at 2 years.

Fire Salamander
(Salamandra salamandra)

Range and habitat: This member of the family Salamandridae is a terrestrial species frequenting woodlands and mossy mountain habitats in southwest Asia and Europe, as well as a small portion of northwestern Africa, (a continent noted for its lack of salamander species). They leave their underground retreats or shelters within decaying logs to forage on wet nights.

Description: The fire salamander, a brilliantly colored creature, is in great demand in the pet trade. The dorsal surface is generally jet black mottled with bright orange or yellow. One closely related species, *Salamandra salamandra fastuosa* is nearly all bright yellow with jet black lines going down the body, legs, and tail. Their common name of fire salamander is not, however, given because of the bright coloration, although it would certainly be suitable. The name apparently arose in Europe from the belief that these creatures were born of fire. Despite its bright coloring, the fire salamander is rarely encountered in the wild, so people living in its habitat were largely unaware of its existence. When logs were brought inside to throw into a fireplace, the heat drove out whatever creatures were sheltering therein. Apparently the most notable, in terms of coloration, were fire salamanders. Since the only time these creatures were seen was during a fire, the superstition arose. The brilliant colors are, of course, a warning

The fire salamander, Salamandra salamandra, *is a spectacularly colored terrestrial species.*

to other creatures that the fire salamander has highly toxic poison glands. The paratoid glands are quite large and noticeable, and smaller glands are spread throughout the skin. When disturbed, this salamander secretes a visible, sticky poison, generally thwarting the efforts of even the most determined predators. This substance would cause great discomfort to a person if it were to get into the eyes or the mouth. Fortunately, these creatures largely give up this habit once accustomed to captivity.

Care: Fire salamanders, which can be bred in captivity, make quite hardy terrarium inhabitants in general; however, a major drawback is their sensitivity to warm temperatures. Most become stressed at temperatures over 70°F (19°C). They will exhibit this by leaving their normal daytime retreats, wandering about the tank and attempting to climb the glass. Skin problems and death will result from sustained temperatures above their preferred range, which is 60 to 65°F (14–16.5°C). Individual fire salamanders have survived for over 50 years

Salamandra salamandra fatuosa shares the fire salamander's coloration, but is striped rather than mottled.

in captivity, which is quite an incredible record for an amphibian. They are stoutly built, and adults can be up to 12 inches (30.4 cm) long. An animal of that size and coloration is quite spectacular. In captivity they exhibit many of the traits that have been described for the tiger salamander, *Ambystoma tigrinum*. They are very visually oriented and seem to anticipate regular feeding times. I have also observed them leave their retreats when they see someone coming near the glass of their terrarium, apparently in anticipation of food. They will feed from the fingers or forceps and are not shy about moving about in broad daylight once they are acclimatized to the captive situation. They are fairly active at night, at least in captivity, and need a good deal of room. It has been said that animals kept in too small quarters will tend to choose the same retreats and pile up together, leading to fungal and other skin problems. A woodland terrarium with a gravel bottom, a water reserve, and a variety of damp retreats is ideal.

Considering their size, one should remember that routine cleaning is necessary. Fire salamanders are probably territorial by nature and will choose the same retreats for a long period of time. Therefore, when cleaning the

tank, their shelters should be returned to the same places each time.

Fire salamanders' appetites are quite easy to satisfy in captivity, although they will accept only living prey. Earthworms, blackworms, slugs, waxworms, crickets, and other small invertebrates are all readily taken. As with many salamanders, adults have a tendency to become obese in captivity. This is not a healthy situation and may interfere with breeding. Adults can be fed three small meals per week or two slightly larger meals.

Breeding: Fire salamanders have a quite unique breeding strategy. They do not lay eggs, but rather give birth to live larvae. Some populations, most notably those living at high elevations, give birth to fully formed small salamanders, skipping the larval stage completely. Depending upon their location within their range, mating takes place in the spring or fall. The male's hold upon the female during the mating process is unique. He slides below her and grasps her from this position with his forelegs. He then holds her above himself in that position for several hours. During this time he is also stimulating her by rubbing the base of his tail on her cloaca and his head on the lower area of her chin. He deposits the spermatophore on land, and the female takes it into her cloaca. The female remains on land within her normal territory until the following breeding season, which would occur in the spring or summer, depending on the range. She then migrates to the water's edge. Generally, a cool pool of water with a high oxygen level is chosen. She stays at the very edge of the water and there deposits up to 70 larvae.

Larvae: The larvae are about 1 inch (2.4 cm) long and are mottled brown and tan with lighter patches at the bases of the limbs. Another unique twist to this strategy is that the larvae are born with four limbs, in contrast to other salamander's larvae, which are limbless when they hatch. They have external gills as do other aquatic salamander larvae. In those populations that give birth on land, the young are fully formed miniatures of the adult, without external gills. Larvae are ravenous and grow quite rapidly. When they transform into the adult stage, their first food can be ten-day-old crickets and blackworms. Larvae can be raised as has been discussed for other typical aquatic salamander larvae—on brine shrimp and chopped blackworms. One might experiment with dried foods also. Terrestrial larvae, that is, those born to females from populations that skip the aquatic stage, can begin feeding on chopped blackworms and pinhead or ten-day-old crickets. As with other salamanders, the larvae will eat nearly every day when growing. This holds true for the terrestrial stage as well as the aquatic. Larvae metamorphose in 2 to 3 months at a size of 1½ to 2 inches (3.8–5 cm). Generally, warmer temperatures will speed metamorphosis. Animals raised at unnaturally high temperatures tend to metamorphose early and at a small size.

Subspecies: Up to eleven subspecies of fire salamander are currently recognized. *Salamandra salamandra terrestris* is found in western Europe. There are also four subspecies on the Iberian Peninsula, one in Corsica, one in North Africa, one in Italy, and two in Asia.

Emperor or Crocodile Newt (*Tylototriton sanjing*)

This colorful member of the Salamandridae family is also referred to as the mandarin newt or the orange-striped newt. While the common name "newt" has taken hold, the animal would more properly be called a salamander. At least in the United States,

"newt" generally indicates an animal that spends most of its life in water, which is not the case for this species. While captive breeding has occurred, most animals that show up in pet stores are wild caught. They are usually extremely stressed by their long journey and by the conditions under which they have been kept.

Range and habitat: The emperor newt is basically terrestrial, being found in wet forests in mountainous areas, occasionally at elevations up to 10,000 feet (3,000 m). Its range covers western Yunan in China, northern India, northern Thailand, and parts of northern Vietnam. These animals spend most of their time underneath rocks, logs, and decaying leaves. In some parts of their range, they appear to be opportunistic breeders, entering small, still pools whenever water is available. These are generally areas with long dry seasons. The eggs are fairly large, considering the size of the animal. Outside of the breeding season, emperor newts are generally active during the wetter times of the year. In those parts of their range that have a distinct wet or monsoon season and a dry season, the entire dry season might be spent in a type of dormancy or aestivation. They are generally fairly inactive animals and their food requirements are correspondingly smaller than would be indicated for a more active animal of similar size. Because of the harsh environments in which they live—dry one part of the year, wet another—these animals can be fairly hardy if kept properly. They are, however, species of high elevations and even though some of the areas in which they occur get quite warm, they seem to be able to control temperatures by burrowing or seeking damp cool places within the habitat.

Description: Adults can reach over 7 inches (18 cm) in length and are

The emperor or crocodile newt, Tylototriton sanjing, *is also called the mandarin or orange-striped newt.*

stoutly built. They appear to be armored, due to bony ridges just below the skin and warty areas that contain the skin toxins.

Care: While there might be a bit of flexibility in their temperature ranges, I would suggest keeping them on the cool side. I am aware of groups maintained year-round at temperatures of 80°F (24°C) and, while they feed and seem to do well, breeding behavior is curtailed and at least those under my observation have seemed not to grow to the full adult size. They are more active and alert and seem to feed better at temperatures of 65 to 70°F (16.5–19°C). Again, this would most likely vary, depending on the part of the range from which the animal originated. As I am uncertain of the origins of the species that I have observed, I cannot draw any conclusions in this regard. Adult mandarin or emperor newts will accept slugs, small snails, earthworms, blackworms, wax-worms, and crickets as food. I have

found that they seem to enter shallow water areas within the terrarium more often than do other terrestrial species; if the water is shallow enough, they will feed there. However, they are not to be housed in deep-water aquariums and will not feed when they are submerged by several inches of water.

Breeding: Breeding has apparently occurred spontaneously in captivity, but a careful look at the climate of the country of origin of the animals would probably be required in order to breed this species regularly. Possibly a dry period followed by a wetter period, or perhaps even a rain system (see page 44), would be required to stimulate the animals to reproduce. Courtship attempts apparently last, in some instances, for several days. Eggs are laid one to two weeks after fertilization. Generally, the eggs are attached to floating objects within the aquarium or to plants or plant roots. The eggs, which are individually attached with threads, will be consumed by the adults if left in the same enclosure.

Larvae: The larvae are tiny, about ½ inch (1.3 cm) in length, and hatch within two to four weeks, depending upon temperature. Daphnia and newly hatched brine shrimp are about the only food items that the larvae are capable of consuming, although finely chopped blackworms might be tried. It may take up to five months for metamorphosis, at which time the granular skin texture and bony ridges begin to become evident.

California Newt
(Taricha torosa)

Range and habitat: Formerly a staple in the pet trade, the California newt is becoming increasingly difficult to find in its natural habitat. Fortunately, these animals can be bred in captivity, but this does not help the natural situation. As this species was once one of the more common inhabitants of the ecosystems in which it occurred, one can assume that the California newt played an important role and affected a great variety of other animals and plants. One of the major threats to the continued survival of the California newt is habitat fragmentation and commercial development. Roads that intersect the migration routes of the California newt are responsible for high mortalities during the breeding season. Along some small stretches of roads, over 200 newts per night are killed. Fortunately, many people are interested in helping this animal. In certain areas crossings have been designed so that the newts are funneled into tunnels dug under the roadways. In one section of California, a short stretch of road is closed throughout the entire migration period, November through March, so that the animals can safely cross. More work is needed to design better systems to funnel larger numbers of newts into protected areas. At these times the

animals are also very susceptible to overcollection for the pet trade, as they are visible in great abundance and unable to escape. Most California newts, especially those from the northern parts of the range, seem to require a winter dormancy for normal behavior and health, not only to stimulate breeding. If not cooled during the winter, it appears that some will not reenter the water in the spring and will refuse to feed at that time.

Description: The California newt is somberly colored above. Generally black to reddish brown, the ventral area is bright orange or bright yellowish in color. The lower eyelid may also be orange. It grows to 7.2 inches (18 cm) in length.

Care: California newts will consume non-living food items during the aquatic phase. When they reemerge onto the land, however, they generally take only

Taricha torosa, the California newt, is becoming rare in its native habitat.

The rough-skinned newt, *Taricha granulosa.*

live food. Reptomin and trout chow will be taken in the water. At other times the animals can be fed blackworms, chopped earthworms, waxworms, and small insects. Studies of wild populations have shown that they are also avid predators upon various types of amphibian eggs and tadpoles. They need to be kept cool, although speci-

mens from the more southern parts of the range are able to tolerate 80°F (24°C) for a couple of months, provided they have access to water. Some individuals can be kept in water year-round; however, to be safe they should be given a choice and their behavior should be carefully monitored. If they appear uncomfortable in water, a more terrestrial woodland-type terrarium is recommended.

Breeding: During the breeding activities, males will grasp the females from above with both legs and will swim off while carrying her if another male approaches. At this time, the male will rub his chin along the female's head and his cloacal area along hers. After a period of time, which may be up to several hours, they will sink to the pond bottom, where the male will crawl over the female and deposit a spermatophore in front of her. She will then take this up into the cloaca and internal fertilization will occur. Clumps of about 30 eggs are attached to underwater structures and the ½ inch-long (1.1 cm) larvae hatch in about two months. Transformation to the adult stage is generally completed within three months. These animals are fairly long lived and do not attain sexual maturity until at least five years of age.

Other species: The closely related rough-skinned newt, *Taricha granulosa,* ranges north to southern Alaska. The belly is yellow to orange and the lower eyelid is dark in contrast to the orange lower eyelid of the California newt. The red-bellied newt, *Taricha rivularis,* is found in northern California. This is a strikingly colored animal, black above with a bright red belly. The lower eyelid is dark.

Crested Newt
(*Triturus cristatus*)
Range and habitat: The crested newt and the closely related members

The red-bellied newt, Taricha rivularis.

of its genus occur in standing and occasionally in flowing waters in central and eastern Europe. Certain species and subspecies occur south to Israel and east to the Ob River and Caspian Sea region. Remember to use caution in handling this and all salamanders. An extremely accomplished animal keeper of my acquaintance inadvertently touched her eye after handling a crested newt. I poured two quarts of saline solution into the eye before the burning sensation ceased.

Description: The crested newt reaches about 6.4 inches (16 cm) in length, is grayish to black above and the ventral area is orange with round black spots. A comblike dorsal crest develops in the males during the breeding season, when they enter the water. In both sexes the tail becomes more paddlelike to facilitate swimming during the breeding seasons, but only the males develop the high showy crest. Certain subspecies develop an incredibly high crest that starts at the nose area and ends at the tail. *Triturus vittatus ophryticus* is particularly well developed in this regard. I have observed *Triturus cristatus* also develop a white line along the sides of the tails of the male, and the females to develop a white line down the back during the breeding season. This white stripe, especially on the tails of the male, is visible from quite a distance, especially when the tail is waved during pheromone dispersal. These colors and the crest are lost after the breeding period, at which time the animals usually return to land. If prevented from returning to land or if kept in very deep water, many will exhibit signs of stress, thrashing about wildly, and eventually may drown. Some races or subspecies, however, can be adapted to a more or less permanent aquatic existence. The only way to be sure of this is to watch the animals carefully.

The crested newt, Triturus cristatus, *native to central and eastern Europe, is found in standing and sometimes in flowing water.*

Care: During the aquatic phase, crested newts will accept nonliving food. In common with many other newts, however, they will generally feed only on living animals once they take up terrestrial existence. Depending upon their origin, crested newts will exhibit different temperature preferences. Most do best if the temperature is kept fairly cool, however. Animals living on land can be housed in a woodland or shoreline terrarium, with access to shallow water at all times. Some aquatic specimens can be kept in water year round; to be safe, however, they should be given a choice and their behavior should be monitored carefully. (See California newt, page 103.)

Breeding: It seems that a change in water depth may bring on the breeding condition at odd times of the year, outside of the normal cycle. In my experience, however, this does not result in a great deal of eggs being produced and the animals quickly return to nonbreeding condition and appearance. Breeding males tend to fight and, although severe damage is rarely inflicted, less dominant animals may become stressed and cease feeding. Courting males position themselves near females and appear to push water containing pheromones toward them with their tails. Females thus stimulated follow the males, push against their tails, and eventually pick up the spermatophore that the male has dropped. Several hundred eggs are laid, each being individually attached to a small water plant. The leaf of the plant is bent around the egg with the female's back legs. Larvae generally hatch within a month and transform into the adult phase during the same summer at a size of 2.4 inches (6 cm). Sexual maturity occurs in about two years depending upon the population.

Captive breeding requires a winter cooling at 36 to 46°F (2 to 8°C). Crested newts, especially the larvae, are particularly sensitive to hygiene and water quality and quick to develop skin problems in suboptimal conditions. They seem very attuned to habitat modifications. As stated earlier, I have observed them come into breeding conditions outside of the breeding season when moved into a larger and deeper aquarium. However, disturbance during the normal breeding season can result in a loss of breeding condition by both sexes.

Sirenidae

Lesser Siren
(Siren intermedia)

Range: Three subspecies of the lesser siren range throughout the southern and central United States.

Description: The western form, *Siren intermedia nettingi,* is the largest, attaining a length of 26 inches (66 cm). The eastern forms are difficult to distinguish from the greater siren, *Siren lacertina;* however, the

lesser siren has 31 to 33 costal grooves, while the greater siren has 36 to 39. The sirens are so unique several taxonomists have considered placing them in their own order. They are totally aquatic and have an eel-like body covered with thick mucus. They exhibit incomplete metamorphosis, retaining the external gills. They lack rear legs, and have only tiny, nearly useless front legs. Sirens are toothless, but the jaws have sharp cutting edges, (rather like a turtle's jaw). Large specimens can bite painfully. Despite the fact that sirens retain external gills, they also develop lungs, which come in handy in the shallow, warm waters that the more southern forms inhabit. Sirens aestivate in those areas of their range where droughts occur. They can survive for up to four months buried in the mud. Under these conditions, the lesser siren forms a protective case around itself, with a small opening by the mouth. This cocoon, comprised of outer skin layers, is formed by multiple sheddings. Parchmentlike in texture, it enables the animal to retain body moisture.

Care: The waters in which sirens occur are generally still, so swift currents within the aquarium are to be avoided. They are best kept in fairly shallow water, generally of a depth in which the siren can rise to the surface to get air without actually having to swim. They do not appear to be active swimmers in the midlayers of the water; rather, they move along the bottom when searching for food. Constant swimming to the top of a deep aquarium might prove stressful to the animal. If the aquarium is fairly deep, you should have dead branches and perhaps tangles of roots, etc., on which the animal can crawl to the top. I have noticed that they will use their small legs to pull themselves along on occasion. In well-oxygenated tanks they

Siren intermedia, *the lesser siren, lacks rear legs and possesses only tiny, almost useless front legs.*

appear to rely mainly on their gills for respiration and I have observed a definite difference in the number of times they rise to the surface for air in an unaerated versus an aerated tank. The western race of the lesser siren remains active and feeding at temperatures of 68°F (20°C) and can tolerate warmer temperatures. One should try to determine the origin of one's animals so that a proper temperature gradient can be provided. Animals from the more northern and perhaps far western parts of the range might need a slight cooling period to stimulate reproduction.

Sirens feed readily on earthworms and blackworms, and particularly relish soft crayfish (that is, crayfish that have recently molted). As with all salamanders, use caution when feeding them crayfish. I generally remove the claws, even though sirens deal with claws in the wild. For smaller sirens,

I prefer to use only newly molted crayfish. I have not observed sirens taking dead prey or pelleted food. They also accept small live minnows, shiners, and tadpoles.

Breeding: The details of siren reproduction are not well known. To my knowledge, they have not reproduced in captivity. Males do not appear to produce a spermatophore as do other salamanders that practice internal fertilization. Studies of their internal anatomies have not revealed the glands that are used to make the covering of a spermatophore. However, eggs are deposited singly or in small clumps. If fertilization were external, as would be indicated by the anatomy of the male, he would have to follow the female for a long period of time and fertilize each egg as it was deposited. This behavior has not been observed among sirens or any of the

The greater siren, Siren lacertina.

dwarf sirens have three fingers on each hand as opposed to four for the other siren species, and the hands are tipped with tiny horny claws, the function of which is as yet unknown. There is only one open gill aperture on the side of the head as opposed to three in the lesser and greater siren. The dwarf sirens, which are native to the southeastern United States, are most abundant in Florida. One theory holds that the dwarf siren's numbers have been boosted by the introduction into the southeastern United States of the water hyacinth, genus *Eichhornia.* This plant appears to provide such an agreeable habitat for the dwarf siren that it has been able to spread into areas where it was not originally found. Water hyacinth is extremely prolific and has become a pest in the South, actually closing down waterways to navigation with its thick growth that covers the surface from shore to shore. The dwarf siren apparently needs low water levels and a good deal of cover. The tangled masses of roots and stems of the water hyacinth provides such cover, and also a microhabitat within deeper water so that the siren can live within a few inches of the surface yet still be in deeper water than it would normally occur. Generally, deep waters lack surface cover and plants that reach from the bottom of the pond to the surface. The water hyacinth provides a highway for the animal to colonize new areas. An incredibly diverse population of invertebrates, amphibians and small fish also inhabit tangled masses of water hyacinths, providing food for the dwarf sirens. In captivity, dwarf sirens require water temperatures of approximately 68°F (20°C), fairly shallow water in depth and with a good deal of cover. If you are able to establish water hyacinths within the aquarium, that might be an ideal situation. Please note that you should check on the

better studied amphibians. Organs that would allow for an as yet undiscovered form of internal fertilization have not been found. Sirens, therefore, present a problem ripe for investigation. This is the sort of research that can make a great impact on the herpetological community, and yet can be carried out by a competent nonprofessional.

Larvae: Lesser siren larvae hatch in approximately two months and are approximately .4 inches (1 cm) long at that time.

Other species: The dwarf siren, *Pseudobranchus striatus,* is an interesting animal and a suitable aquarium inhabitant. It is similar to the other sirens in general body form, but is much smaller, reaching a maximum size of only 8.5 inches (21 cm). The coloring is also different. They are dark brown with one to four light stripes along the back and two broader stripes along the sides. Sometimes these stripes are almost yellow in color. There are five subspecies, mainly differentiated by the pattern of striping. Another way to distinguish the dwarf siren from the larger species is that the legality of keeping this plant. Many states have outlawed its sale due to the potential for it to become a pest as it has in the Southeast. I have observed it in ponds in New York, far north of its natural habitat. An ideal substitute would be devil's ivy, which grows well in shallow, aerated water and produces tangled root and stem masses much like hyacinth. The leaves covering the surface will also cut down on light levels below the water, creating a more comfortable environment for the sirens. As with all aquatic salamanders, careful attention should be paid to water quality, and water used in the aquarium should be free of chlorine and chloramine.

Amphiumidae

In the amphiuma family one finds creatures that appear to be far removed from salamanders in both appearance and behavior. The amphiumas are eel-like in appearance, darkly colored and with a great deal of mucus on the skin. They have four tiny limbs that are only evident upon close examination, and that are, it seems, useless to the animal. Each limb has one to three toes, depending upon the species. All three of the amphiuma species are entirely aquatic, although the two-toed and the three-toed amphiumas will occasionally leave the water on wet nights to travel to new areas, and at egg-laying time. The tiny eyes are covered with skin and lack lids. In feeding, they appear to use the sense of smell and also respond rapidly to touch—for example, if the end of their body rubs against a food item, they will instantly dart back and grab it. Upon hatching, the larvae have external gills, but lose them quickly, usually within two or three months. One pair of gill slits is evident on the adults, but respiration is via their lungs and skin. Amphiumas lay bead-like strings of eggs, up to 200 for large animals, in a muddy depression below some sort of cover such as a log or a board. The nesting area itself may actually be out of the water, but the eggs are generally in the water that collects in the bottom of the depression hollowed out by the female. Fertilization is internal. The female guards the eggs until they hatch. Little is known about her behavior during this time. For example, it is uncertain whether she stays with the eggs during the entire period or leaves to feed on occasion. Incubation, at least in the two larger species, takes five months.

Three-toed amphiuma
(Amphiuma tridactylum)

Range: This animal's range extends from western Alabama into Texas and north to southeastern Missouri and Kentucky. Mating occurs from December to June. Nests have been observed from April through October. As with the other two amphiuma species, it spends the day buried in the mud or below a shelter, and

Amphiuma tridactylum, *the three-toed amphiuma.*

emerges at night to actively search for food.

The three-toed amphiuma was said to have been an important dietary item for certain Native Americans, and although I do not have any details, I have heard that they are still eaten in parts of their range. It is also said that they are frequently caught on fishing lines and that most people cut the line upon seeing what is at the end of it.

Description: The three-toed amphiuma can reach 41¾ inches (106 cm) in length.

Care: There is little that the three-toed amphiumas will pass up in the way of food, so it is fairly easy to give them a varied and potentially well-rounded diet. Mine have done well for years on whole fish, earthworms, blackworms, recently molted crayfish, tadpoles, and an occasional pink mouse. Extreme care must be exercised when placing your hand into the aquarium for cleaning or feeding purposes. In very unsalamander-like fashion, they respond with lightning speed to water movement nearby, strike out, and latch onto whatever gets in their way. They seem not to check for size of the prey item, but rather bite first. The powerful jaws and sharp teeth can inflict painful wounds. It is a good idea to use tongs to make sure that all animals in the tank are feeding and that biting does not occur during the feeding process. However, hard metal tongs will be grabbed very quickly, and may possibly injure the animal. Be sure to hold the prey item well back to be certain that the animal grabs the food and not the tongs.

Although the three-toed and other amphiumas appear to occur in fairly acidic waters in the wild state, this should not be taken as an invitation to ignore water quality. Ammonia buildup within the tank will kill these animals as it will any other salamander. Due to their large size and voracious eating habits, frequent water changes are required. Because they are very active swimmers at night, any tank decorations must be heavy and securely fastened. Amphiumas are also escape artists, and in their nocturnal prowling will certainly push up against the screen top of an aquarium and escape if able. While they can survive some drying, death from desiccation will eventually occur. And who knows what mayhem they might inflict on the hapless kitten or puppy that gets in their way while they are trying to make good their escape!

Two-toed amphiuma
(*Amphiuma means*)

Range: The two-toed amphiuma ranges along the east coast, mainly within the coastal plain area from southern Virginia to Florida and into eastern Louisiana. Eggs are laid in June and July in the northern part of the range, and January through February in the southernmost areas. This animal is as quick to bite as the three-toed, and has been observed feeding on small snakes.

Description: Largest of the three species, *Amphiuma means* measures up to 45¾ inches (116.2 cm) in

Amphiuma means, the two-toed amphiuma.

length. It may be distinguished from the other large species by the presence of two as opposed to three toes on each of the four tiny limbs. It appears that the two-toed and three-toed amphiumas occasionally interbreed where their range overlaps, and some authorities consider them to be a single species. When properly maintained, they can live a rather long time; one two-toed amphiuma was kept for twenty-seven years in captivity.

Breeding: While the keeping of the two large species of amphiumas is not all that difficult if one can give proper attention to water quality and has the space required for such large animals, breeding in captivity is another matter. Because they change habitats for breeding, one must be able to move the animals or to change their setup to stimulate breeding. A temperature and light regimen should be established following the pattern of the area in which the animal lives. At the appropriate time of the year, one might try dropping the water level and creating a muddy bank area with debris under which these animals can burrow. A children's wading pool or something a little larger would be ideal for this. Bear in mind that a suitable cover must be fashioned, however.

One-toed amphiuma
(Amphiuma pholeter)
Description: The one-toed amphiuma is the smallest and least known of the three species. It reaches only 13 inches (31 cm) in length, and its breeding habits have been little studied. Far more secretive than the others, it spends a good deal of its time burrowed in the mud, in a hole of its own making or that of some other animal.

Range: Amphiuma pholeter is found in the Florida Panhandle, the Gulf Hammock region, and southeastern Georgia.

Proteidae

Mudpuppy
(Necturus maculosus)
Range and habitat: The mudpuppy ranges from southwestern Manitoba and southern Quebec to Georgia and Louisiana. Human introductions are responsible for disjunct populations in several large rivers in the northeastern areas of its range. The various subspecies occupy a wide variety of habitats, ranging from still, shallow swamps to deep, cold lakes and swiftly flowing rivers.

Description: The mudpuppy is one of our largest salamanders, commonly reaching 13 inches (33 cm) in length. The record is 17 inches (40.8 cm). A large adult is quite a bizarre and striking creature, especially to the unwary fisherman who reels one up on his line for the first time. As they are completely aquatic and nocturnal, this is generally the way they are discovered. The body is flattened to facilitate the animal's living under stones and logs, and the slime covering is profuse. The gills are external. Body coloration is

The mudpuppy, Necturus maculosus, *is one of the largest North American salamanders.*

111

A close up of the mudpuppy showing its reddish gills.

nant waters generally have large gills to facilitate oxygen uptake. Those from fast-moving streams have smaller gills that are closer to the head, as the oxygen content is generally higher in such waters. Mudpuppies also possess lungs and can rise to the surface to breathe. The name mudpuppy or waterdog seems to have arisen from the mistaken belief that these animals bark. Also, at a certain angle the wide head appears somewhat doglike. They are always found in permanent bodies of water, most generally those with a higher oxygen content, and often in moving streams or rivers. This is a general rule however, and especially in the South, slower, more quiet bodies of water are inhabited. The northern mudpuppy exists in several races or subspecies. One, the Lake Winnebago mudpuppy, *Necturus maculosus stictus,* is very large and dark gray to almost black in color. It is found in northeastern Wisconsin and Michigan. One individual was collected at a water depth of 90 feet (27 m).

rust brown, occasionally almost reddish, to gray, with a pattern of blue-black dots and blotches. It is sturdily built with a wide head and tiny eyes. The legs, which are fairly small and suitable for crawling along the bottom, do not assist in swimming. The size of the gills depends upon the animal's habitat. Those from slower, more stag-

Care: The mudpuppy consumes nearly any small creature that it can overpower. Many populations are said to live chiefly on crayfish, and I have observed most to be extremely fond of this food item. I generally use very small animals with the claws removed, or newly shed individuals. Other food favorites include earthworms, black-worms, small fish, and tadpoles. They are extremely sensitive to high light levels and will be very difficult to observe in a brightly lit aquarium. Hiding places are essential, even for most well-habituated individuals. If given hiding places and dim lighting, however, they will often emerge during the day to feed. While I have only observed them feeding upon living prey, I have been told by reliable sources that they will consume trout chow, even learning to swim to the surface for it. As I have had good

Necturus punctatus, *the dwarf water dog.*

success using trout chow with other large aquatic salamanders, it might make a good diet for mudpuppies as well. Mudpuppies are best kept in very large, well-filtered aquariums. An under gravel filter, perhaps with an external filter as well, is the best choice for filtration. While they can rise to the surface for air, they do better in well-aerated tanks so that they can remain on the bottom and use their gills for breathing. They do not seem comfortable leaving their shelters and swimming to the surface, especially in large aquariums. The northern races are generally found in cool water and this should be provided in captivity as well. As with most large aquatic amphibians, waste products are fairly toxic when released from the body; therefore, it is important that filtration be strong and that regular water changes are performed. These animals are fairly sensitive to poor water quality. Water should also be dechlorinated before being added to the aquarium.

Breeding: Captive breeding, while not common, has been accomplished. These animals become sexually mature at four to six years of age. A cavity below a rock or log is chosen for the site of egg laying. The eggs are laid individually and take anywhere from six to ten weeks to develop. The female guards the eggs during the entire time of incubation. Detailed observations on this behavior—for example whether or not she leaves to feed and how she reacts to threats—would be most interesting.

Larvae: Larvae are nearly 1 inch (2.5 cm) long when they hatch, which makes feeding easier, as they can take chopped blackworms right away. They are, however, highly predacious upon each other and need to be separated or kept in very large tanks with a good deal of cover and a constant supply of food.

Necturus lewisi, *the Neuse River water dog.*

Other species: In addition to the various races of the northern mudpuppy, there are several other species including the Gulf Coast waterdog, *Necturus beyeri,* which grows only to the length of 8.8 inches (22 cm) and is restricted in range to flowing waters from eastern Texas to central Louisiana. The dwarf waterdog, *Necturus punctatus,* matures at a length

Necturus alabamensis, *the Alabama water dog.*

113

of 4½ to 6½ inches (11.4–16.5 cm), and is found in the southeastern United States, on the coastal plain from southern Virginia to south-central Georgia. It can occasionally be found in quite sluggish or even still water. The Neuse River waterdog, *Necturus lewisi,* is restricted to the Neuse and Tar Rivers in North Carolina, and the Alabama waterdog, *Necturus alabamensis,* occurs in central Georgia through the Florida Panhandle. Both of these animals are fairly small as compared to the northern mudpuppy, reaching only 8 to 9 inches (20.3–22.9 cm) in length.

The Olm
(Proteus anguineus)

Range and habitat: In natural circumstances olms seem never to enter into daylight or above the ground at all. Their entire habitat seems to be underground lakes and streams, in a restricted area from the Eastern Alps in Austria through Trieste and into western Yugoslavia. The areas in which they are found are mainly limestone mountains, so the waters they inhabit are fairly high in calcium content and therefore hard, with a pH of about 6.3. The waters are also well oxygenated. Having evolved in such a very unique habitat, olms are extremely sensitive to any changes to their wild or captive environment. It should be remembered, too, that the system of caves in which they live seems to be fairly germ-free, and that the animals have most likely very little in the way of natural defenses to bacteria and viruses. Young olms have never been found in the wild. They seem to live deep within the cave system. Most of what is known about them has been discovered by biologists working in laboratories under special conditions.

Description: The olm is among the strangest of all salamanders, if not of all animals. The animal has an elongated shape. Tiny, degenerated eyes are hidden beneath skin. The legs are weakly developed. The hands have three fingers, the feet two toes, and the reddish gills are external. One subspecies, *P.a. parkelj,* has been identified. It is black, and apparently has well-developed eyes.

Care: Olms have very primitive, poorly developed lungs and external gills. Even in oxygen-rich water, they appear to come to the surface regularly for air. They have been observed to leave the water, and even to feed on land. Whether or not this occurs in the wild is uncertain. Being creatures of complete darkness, they are extremely sensitive to and disturbed by light and in captivity they will become sick and die if suddenly forced to live in bright conditions. However, it seems that they can be gradually habituated to light, will actually darken in color, and begin to act normally in the presence of direct sunlight. When returned to darkness, their coloration fades. While they have experimentally endured higher temperatures, olms are adapted to and do best at 42.8 to 53.6°F (6–12°C). In the wild they appear to feed mainly on tiny cave-dwelling crustaceans. Strangely enough, considering the delicate nature of these animals and the strict habitat requirements that they impose on their keepers, specimens in European collections have lived for at least 15 years and have reproduced regularly. While collecting should be completely prohibited, this is an animal that needs a great deal of study in captivity and one that the interested person who has the proper facilities should strive to work with. An ideal situation to me would seem to be a Living Stream setup (see page 28). These large trout-holding tanks are refrigerated and allow for a strong water current. Limestone rocks could be used to form the cave system preferred by these animals. The motors on living streams are powerful enough to pump water through channels within the rock, as might occur in the natural situation. Of course, strict attention must be paid to hygiene, water chemistry, and illumination.

Breeding: Mature males who are courting females, at least in captivity, stake out a territory and will attack any other male entering. Injuries from the fights are often serious. Gravid females also establish a territory that they defend against all intruders. It seems that males, in captivity at least, have also been observed to guard eggs. Females have been observed moving eggs about with their mouths, but the purpose of this is not yet known. Stranger still is their habit of occasionally giving birth to live young. The normal breeding strategy is as yet unknown or perhaps the animals can somehow switch their mode of giving birth depending upon what circumstances within their habitat dictate. The eggs generally take about two months to hatch in the cool temperatures at which olms live, and sexual maturity is not reached for at least two years. Up to 75 eggs have been laid by a single female over a period of one month. Larvae hatch out at about .8 inches (2 cm) in length. Fully grown adults are 11.2 inches (28 cm) long.

Cryptobranchidae

Hellbender
(Cryptobranchus alleganiensis)
Range and habitat: The hellbender ranges from the Susquehanna River drainage in southeastern New York to the headwaters of the Chesapeake Bay (the fresh water sections), and to southern Illinois and northeast Mississippi. There are disjunct populations in the northern parts of Alabama and Georgia and in central and southwestern Missouri. It possibly occurs in some locations in Kansas as well. Despite this large range, the animal is in extreme danger of becoming extinct in many areas. Within this large range it is completely restricted to clean, cool flowing rivers and streams, generally with a rocky bottom and containing large hiding places such as flat rocks and logs. Studies have shown that hellbender population densities are directly linked to the availability of suitable shelters. The rivers and streams in which they live have fast-moving water in general and are usually devoid of cover, except for large structures such as big flat rocks, tree stumps, or fallen trees. Such waters are generally cool and, in the natural state, clean and fairly stable chemically. Hellbenders are among the first creatures affected by the introduction of pollutants into the ecosystem. They have been found in quite shallow water, as long as there is appropriate cover, and range commonly into water 5 feet (1.5 m) deep as well.

Description: The hellbender is the American representative of the family Cryptobranchidae, which includes the 5-foot (152 cm) long Japanese giant salamander, *Andrias japonicas* and Chinese giant salamander *Andrias davidianu*. While the hellbender does not approach those lengths, it is quite certainly a giant among American salamanders, nearly the longest and certainly the heaviest. Routinely growing to a length of 11½ to 20 inches (29–51 cm), a record 29⅛ inch (74 cm) female has been found. They are interesting in appearance to say the least. They have been known to grab fishing lines and people unfamiliar with them will often cut the line rather than deal with this imposing beast. The flattened head and body, which are quite wide, have fleshy folds of skin along their sides. The skin is thick and there are longitudinal furrows along the throat. The eyes are tiny, lidless, and nearly

The hellbender, Cryptobranchus alleganiensis, *is nearly the longest and certainly the heaviest of American salamanders.*

invisible. They are located on top of the head. It is probable that the hellbender cannot form very distinct images, but senses light and dark only.

Recent work has shown that the entire skin surface of this giant salamander is light-sensitive and it appears that the sensitivity is greater in the tail and lower body region. The theory is that this would warn the creature when its tail and lower part of the body were exposed from its rock hideaway and therefore subject to predation.

Like many aquatic salamanders, hellbenders possess a lateral line organ system similar to that used by fish. This seems to help them sense water vibrations and possibly to orient themselves toward or away from predators or food items. Even within the same river, the coloration of individual hellbenders varies a great deal. Dull brown is the most common color, but there are

many gray animals and some are olive green or even orange and reddish. There is usually a form of washed-out spotted or mottled, darker pattern.

Care: Hellbenders must be kept in well-oxygenated water; even though the lungs could be used for respiration, the animals would be extremely stressed having to leave their hideaways and rise to the surface for air. Hellbenders are only truly at home in very spacious containers in which they can be completely hidden most of the time. Well-adjusted animals might venture out on occasion to feed, but they are generally fairly secretive in nature. The animals will do well in a bare-bottom tank, preferably a large refrigerated one with a powerful filtration system such as a Living Stream. Filtration should be through activated carbon. Strict attention must be paid to hygiene, with frequent water changes being the rule. These are quite large animals that produce copious waste products. Being in liquid form, however, these wastes are not always evident. Hellbenders are extremely sensitive to additives to the water, so care should be taken to use only decholorinated water. Spring water, although expensive, would probably be the safest way to go when keeping hellbenders. Captive breeding has occurred, but it is the exception rather than the rule. Once adjusted to captivity, hellbenders can do quite well if their requirements are met, and one animal has survived for over 30 years in captivity. Light levels should be kept low.

They do best at cool temperatures, with 60 to 65°F (14–16.5°C) being safe for most populations. Some experimentation is required regarding cooling as a therapeutic measure. As mentioned earlier, cool temperatures seem to stimulate the healing process in certain amphibians. I am aware of two cases of hellbenders that were apparently dead and placed into a refrigerator awaiting necropsy. To the owner's surprise, the animals were moving about in the morning and in one case the animal lived for several years, apparently "healed" by the 40°F (4°C) temperature inside the refrigerator.

Studies of free-living animals have shown that crayfish are a staple in the diet, and captives certainly relish this food item. Aquatic insects are also taken, as are snails, small fish, earthworms, and blackworms.

The hellbender is one of the few salamanders that can inflict a painful bite. While they do not warrant the fear that many people feel toward them, one should be careful in handling them as they resent this process violently. Also, hungry animals will snap at anything that moves past their shelter, so take extreme care when working in their aquarium with your hands. The skin is extremely sensitive and easily damaged by nylon nets. Ushering the animal into a plastic bucket is a safer way of moving them when necessary.

Breeding: A careful study should be made of the animal's natural habitat so that light requirements, daylight length, and temperature can be adjusted to induce breeding. A large enclosure should be provided, and the male should be given the opportunity to choose from several nest sites. A strong water flow might be necessary to stimulate the male to breed or to choose a site. As the nest opening always faces downstream, a similar situation should be created in the terrarium. Females introduced into the aquarium should be removed after egg laying, as the male will then defend the eggs from them and anything else in the tank. In contrast to most other salamanders, hellbenders practice external fertilization. The male hollows out a nest in the river bottom, always under a protective rock or some other source of cover. The opening of the nest always faces downstream. Males corral gravid females that pass by, then herd them into the nest. There is no amplexus. Upon the female's release of her eggs, the male ejects sperm into the water over the eggs. Usually the male will have the eggs of several females in his nest.

Larvae: Larvae hatch out at the relatively large size of 1.2 inches (3 cm) in about 10 to 12 weeks. They lose their external gills at a size of approximately 4 inches (10 cm) long. They are fairly slow growing and it takes about three years to reach this stage. Sexual maturity is not attained until at least five years of age, possibly much longer. Adult hellbenders retain certain larval characteristics such as certain aspects of dentition and the lack of eyelids. They do develop lungs, but do not seem to often use them for

along the bottom. Perhaps their flattened appearance is an adaptation for moving about along the bottom of the often swift-moving rivers that they inhabit. The lungs appear to be involved in buoyancy control. Their appearance and development has caused a great deal of discussion and confusion, especially regarding respiration. In fact, the name *Cryptobranchus* means "hidden gills". Adults retain gill slits where the gills were located on the larvae. Early researchers assumed the openings were connected to internal gills and that respiration occurred in that manner. It now seems that most respiration is cutaneous, that is, it occurs through the skin. The many loose folds of skin along the body and head increase the surface area for absorption of oxygen.

Subspecies: One subspecies of hellbender has been described. The Ozark hellbender, *Cryptobranchus alleganiensis bishopi,* has larger, darker blotches on its back than does the hellbender, and the lower lips are heavily spotted with black in contrast to the lightly spotted or unspotted lips of the hellbender. This animal is confined to portions of the Black River and the north fork of the White River in southeastern Missouri and Arkansas.

respiration, as they are very rarely observed to surface for air either in the natural or captive situation. They remain as completely aquatic animals and are virtually helpless on land. Despite their aquatic existence, they do not actually swim much, but crawl

Appendix: Diseases of Newts and Salamanders

Symptoms	Possible Causes	Diagnosis
General		
anorexia	behavioral	review husbandry
	foreign body	gastric wash
	infections, toxins	x-ray, endoscope
weight loss	mycobacterial infection	x-ray, CBC
	fungal	cloacal culture, liver biopsy
lethargy, nonresponsive	environmental factors, nutrition, infection	review husbandry, diet cultures
edema, ascites	viral, bacterial	culture lymph, CBC,
	water quality	chemistries, test water
	parasites, organ failure	
Skin		
erosion/ulceration	bacterial, fungal, mycobacterial infection, parasites	culture, biopsy lesion, acid fast and Gram's stain of cutaneous swab
	chemical insult	
discoloration	behavioral, chromomycosis	cutaneous swab for cytology,
	algae, trematodes	check water
edema	tadpole edema virus	check water quality
	water osmolarity changes	culture, necropsy
	bacterial infection	histopathology
	renal failure	
(cottony) material	funal (*Saproiegnia*) infection	culture, cytology of cutaneous swab
nodular mass	mycobacterial infection	needle aspirate, biopsy, acid
	parasitic granuloma	fast stain, culture, cytology
	bacterial abscess, neoplasia	
Musculoskeletal		
spindly legs	nutritional deficiency	no cure, provide balanced diet to adults
deformed/soft bones	calcium:phosphorus imbalance	x-ray
	vitamin D deficiency	review diet, husbandry, replace
	UV light deficiency	UV bulbs
	congenital defects	
weakness	nutritional deficiency	review diet, biopsy, necropsy
	generalized infection	
nodular masses	parasites, bacterial abscesses	biopsy, culture, acid fast stains
	mycobacterial abscesses	x-ray
	neoplasia	
fractures	trauma, nutritional deficiency	x-ray, review diet
Gastrointestinal		
regurgitation	parasites	gastric wash, cytology
	foreign bodies	endoscopy, x-ray,
	bacterial infections	fecal exam for parasites
diarrhea	bacterial infection	cloacal culture, fecal exam
	parasites	for parasites
	toxic insult	check water quality

Adapted from "Amphibians" by Dr. Bonnie Raphael (*Exotic Pet Medicine*, 23(6):1271, 1993).

Plethodon yonahlossee, *a species found only in the mountains of eastern Tennessee and western North Carolina.*

A head-on view of a hellbender, Crytobranchus alleganiensis.

Pseudotriton ruber vioscai, *a subspecies of the northern red salamander.*

An emperor (or crocodile) newt, Tylototriton shanjing *(formerly called* Tylototriton verrucosus).

A subspecies of the fire salamander, Salamandra salamandra fatuosa, *spectacularly displayed against a green leaf.*

A pair of Spanish ribbed newts, Pleurodeles waltl, *in amplexus.*

Gyrinophilus porphyriticus danielsi, *a subspecies of the spring salamander.*

Developing axolotl larva, Ambystoma mexicanum, *in an egg capsule.*

The spotted salamander, Ambystoma maculatum, *in its forest habitat.*

A close-up of Aneides aeneus, *the green salamander.*

121

Glossary

adaptation features of an animal that assist its survival in a particular environment. Adaptations may be genetic or behavioral.

aestivate to enter a state of reduced activity during hot, dry weather.

amplexus amphibian mating position (used by most frogs and many salamanders) during which the male clasps the female with one or two pairs of legs.

aquatic living mainly in the water.

arboreal living mainly in trees.

chemosensation detection of particular chemicals in the environment.

cloaca common opening into which the reproductive and digestive tracts empty.

clutch total number of eggs laid during one breeding episode.

cold-blooded see endothermic.

courtship behavioral displays and interactions that occur before and during the mating process.

cutaneous respiration transfer of oxygen and carbon dioxide through the skin.

ectothermic animals whose bodily temperature varies with that of the external environment. Formerly referred to as *cold-blooded*.

eft immature, land-dwelling stage in the life cycle of a newt.

environment all of the factors (thermal, chemical, psychological, etc.) that affect an animal.

external fertilization union of egg and sperm outside the body of the female.

gestation period of development of the offspring that occurs inside the body of the female.

gular pertaining to the throat.

habitat physical characteristics of the area in which an organism lives.

hybrid offspring derived from the mating of two animals of different species.

internal fertilization union of egg and sperm inside the body of the female.

Jacobsen's organ (vomeronasal organ) structure in some mammals, reptiles, and amphibians that allows for chemosensation of particular molecules in the environment.

larva early, immature form in the development of salamanders and certain other animals.

lateral line arrangement of sense organs in the skin of certain aquatic animals that allows for the detection of water-borne vibrations and, possibly, chemosensation.

leucistic pertaining to the condition (caused by genetic mutation) in which normal pigments are absent. The animal is white, but may also have certain areas of normal coloration.

metamorphosis transformation, usually involving a change in appearance, from one stage of an animal's life to another.

neotenic retaining larval characteristics in sexually mature animals.

nuptial pads roughened areas that develop on the forearms of some male amphibians during the breeding season. The pads assist the male in grasping the female during amplexus.

olfactory pertaining to the sense of smell.

paedomorphic see neotonic.

paratoid gland protrusions on the skin of certain amphibians that contain toxins used to discourage, injure, or kill predators.

permeable characteristic of a surface that allows for the passage of certain substances.

pheromones chemical secretions that communicate messages to other animals—such as readiness to breed or claim to a territory.

population group of animals of the same species that occupy a particular area.

race a taxonomic grouping below the subspecies level. Animals of the same race share certain characteristics that differentiate them from others of their species or subspecies.

range geographic area within which an organism is found.

sexual dimorphism physical characteristics that differentiate the sexes.

spermatophore packet containing sperm, which the female takes into her body.

substrate substance, such as wood, rock, or moss, on which an organism dwells.

subspecies distinct group of animals within a species, often inhabiting a range isolated from other members of the species.

terrestrial living chiefly on the land.

tubercle a projection from the skin of an animal. Burrowing salamanders frequently have tubercles on their feet to assist in digging.

vomeronasal see Jacobsen's organ.

Useful Literature and Addresses

Books and Articles

Behler, J. L. *The Audubon Society Field Guide to North American Reptiles and Amphibians*. New York: Knopf, 1979.

Burton, M. (ed.). *The New Larousse Encyclopedia of Animal Life*. New York: Bonanza Books, 1981.

Cogger, Dr. H. G., and Zweifel, Dr. R. G. (eds.). *Reptiles and Amphibians*. New York: Smithmark, 1992.

Conant, R. *A Field Guide to Reptiles and Amphibians of Eastern North America*. Boston: Houghton Mifflin, 1958.

Duellman, W. E., and Trueb, L. *Biology of Amphibians*. New York: McGraw-Hill, 1986.

Grzimek, B. (ed.). *Grzimek's Animal Life Encyclopedia, Vol 5., Fishes II and Amphibians*. New York: Van Nostrand-Reinhold Co., 1984.

Halliday, Dr. T., and Adler, Dr. K. *The Encyclopedia of Reptiles and Amphibians*. New York: Facts on File, 1986.

Hoff, G. L., Frye, F. L. and Jacobson, E. R. (eds.). *Diseases of Amphibians and Reptiles*. New York: Plenum, 1984.

Klingenberg, Dr. R. J. *Understanding Reptile Parasites*. Lakeside: Advanced Vivarium Systems, 1993.

Murphy, J. B., Adler, K., and Collins, J. T. *Captive Management and Conservation of Amphibians and Reptiles*. Ithaca: Society for the Study of Amphibians and Reptiles, 1994.

Raphael, Dr. B. L. "Amphibians," *Exotic Pet Medicine*, 23(6): 1271. 1993.

Stebbins, R. C. *A Field Guide to Reptiles and Amphibians of Western North America*. Boston: Houghton Mifflin, 1966.

Stebbins, R. C., and Cohen, N. W. *A Natural History of Amphibians*. Princeton: Princeton University Press, 1995.

Magazines and Journals

Copeia
American Society of Ichthyologists and Herpetologists
810 East 10 Street
P.O. Box 1897
Lawrence, Kansas 66044

Ambystoma maculatum, *the spotted salamander.*

Herpetologica
Herpetologist's League
Department of Biological Sciences
Box 70726
East Tennessee State University
Johnson City, Tennessee 37614-0736

Journal of Herpetology
Society for the Study of Amphibians
    and Reptiles
Department of Zoology
Ohio University
Athens, Ohio 45701

Reptile and Amphibian Magazine
Remus Publishing, Inc.
RD no. 3
Box 37709-A
Pottsville, Pennsylvania 17901

Reptiles Magazine
Fancy Publications, Inc.
P.O. Box 58700
Boulder, Colorado 80322

The Vivarium
American Federation of
    Herpetologists
120 West Grand Street
Escondido, California 92025

Societies and Organizations
American Museum of Natural History
Central Park West and 79 Street
New York, New York 10024

American Zoo Association
Oglebay Park
Wheeling, West Virginia 26003-1698
    Sponsors regional and national
meetings and publishes a monthly
bulletin concerning all aspects of zoo
and aquarium operation.

Bronx Zoo/Wildlife Conservation Park
185 Street and Southern Boulevard
Bronx, New York 10460
    Membership includes a magazine,
travel opportunities, and invitations to
special events. A separate newsletter
is available to those who support projects sponsored by the Department of
Herpetology.

New York Herpetological Society
P.O. Box 1245
Grand Central Station
New York, New York 10163-1245
    Like many local herpetological soci-
eties, the NYHS hosts monthly meetings, sponsors field trips, sponsors a
rescue network, and is involved in
local environmental issues.

Science Development, Inc.
400 Riverside Drive
Suite 4A
New York, New York 10025
    Provides science programs, taught by
recognized experts, to schools, teachers'
groups, and other organizations.

Index

Numerals in **bold type** indicate color photos. **C1** designates front cover; **C2**, inside front cover; **C3**, inside back cover; **C4**, back cover.